CULTURE SMART!

# RWANDA

Brian Crawford

·K·U·P·E·R·A·R·D·

ISBN 978 1 85733 879 9

British Library Cataloguing in Publication Data
A CIP catalogue entry for this book is available from the British Library

First published in Great Britain
by Kuperard, an imprint of Bravo Ltd
59 Hutton Grove, London N12 8DS
Tel: +44 (0) 20 8446 2440  Fax: +44 (0) 20 8446 2441
www.culturesmart.co.uk
Inquiries: sales@kuperard.co.uk

Series Editor  Geoffrey Chesler
Design  Bobby Birchall

Printed in the USA

## About the Author

BRIAN CRAWFORD is a multiple-award-winning teacher and the author of fourteen novels. His first, *The Weaver's Scar: For Our Rwanda* (Royal Fireworks Press, 2013), is the first young-adult English-language novel dealing directly with the 1994 Rwandan genocide. It received two prestigious awards: the Skipping Stones Honor Award for Multicultural and International Books (2014), and the VOYA Top Shelf Fiction Award (2014). Brian has traveled many times to Rwanda, where he has coordinated educational partnerships between Rwandan and American schools. He has supported Intore Expeditions' Kids to the Parks program, which raises money to send Rwandan students to visit their own national parks. Brian holds a dual M.A. in French Literature and Modern German Culture from Indiana University. He speaks six languages, including conversational Kinyarwanda. Brian currently lives in Seattle, Washington.

The publishers would like to thank **CultureSmart!**Consulting for its help in researching and developing the concept for this series.

**CultureSmart!**Consulting creates tailor-made seminars and consultancy programs to meet a wide range of corporate, public-sector, and individual needs. Whether delivering courses on multicultural team building in the USA, preparing Chinese engineers for a posting in Europe, training call-center staff in India, or raising the awareness of police forces to the needs of diverse ethnic communities, it provides essential, practical, and powerful skills worldwide to an increasingly international workforce.

For details, visit www.culturesmartconsulting.com

**CultureSmart!**Consulting and **CultureSmart!** guides have both contributed to and featured regularly in the weekly travel program "Fast Track" on BBC World TV.

# contents

# contents

# Map of Rwanda

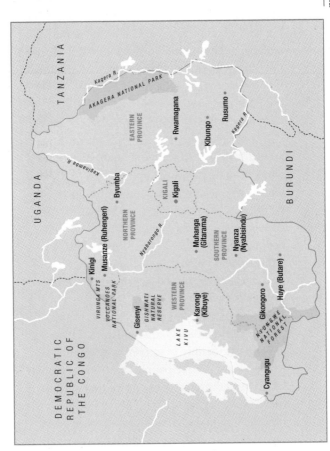

# introduction

Known as "The Land of a Thousand Hills," Rwanda is a land of powerful images. It is the home of the endangered mountain gorilla, lumbering through the thick vegetation of the Virunga Mountains. It is a place of abundant natural beauty—both in the rainforest of the western perimeter, and in the dazzling display of wildlife. It is a land of tea, coffee, and intricately woven baskets; of drumming, artistic, and skillful Intore dancers, waving their white headdresses about and brandishing spears and shields. It has a growing film industry, a world-renowned cycling team, and a thriving contemporary music scene. The economy is burgeoning, and the capital, Kigali, glimmers almost weekly with new construction.

Despite its breathtaking growth, Rwanda's international image was greatly tarnished by the 1994 Genocide of the Tutsi, perhaps the most efficient genocide in human history. This dark chapter is indelibly ingrained in the national psyche, and both the people and the government have worked tirelessly to ensure that such a horror never again occurs. The economy has been reborn; Rwandans have embraced forgiveness, reconciliation, and restorative justice as a path to heal old wounds; former "ethnic" labels have been effaced in favor of a unified Rwandan identity;

and, according to the World Economic Forum, the country has become the ninth-safest in the world for tourists and businesses. Of course, some individuals, scholars, and international organizations have questioned the manner in which unity has been achieved, the freedom of political discourse, or the nature of democracy in contemporary Rwanda. There is a high level of security and stability, they point out, but at what cost?

Whatever the political reality, the Rwandans remain a dignified, reserved, and welcoming people. They harbor a deep pride in their common culture and history, which they are happy to showcase to the inquisitive visitor. Whether cultivating the land, building new infrastructure, positioning Rwanda as a high-end tourist destination, or developing the country as an investment and ICT hub for Eastern Africa, Rwandans are dedicated to development. But to make the most of your stay here, plunge below superficial interactions. Talk to the local people at home, at work, at leisure, and in Kinyarwanda, their own language. By making the effort to meet them on their own terms, you will find that you can make lifelong friends in a land steeped in a unique history and culture. You will discover why, according to the local proverb, Rwanda is where God comes to sleep at night.

# Key Facts

| | | |
|---|---|---|
| **Official Name** | Republic of Rwanda | Republika y'uRwanda |
| **Capital City** | Kigali | Pop. approx. 1 million |
| **Area** | 10,169 sq. mi. (26,338 sq. km.) | Comparable in size to Wales or the US state of Maryland |
| **Geography** | Bordered by Uganda, Tanzania, Burundi, Democratic Republic of the Congo, and Lake Kivu | The Kagera River forms the eastern border with Tanzania. |
| **Regions** | Five provinces: Kigali City, Eastern (Est), Northern (Nord), Western (Ouest), and Southern (Sud) | |
| **Terrain** | Mountainous in the west with dense jungles in the northwest and the southwest. The terrain gradually flattens from west to east, where it opens up to savannah. Papyrus swamps are common around lakes and rivers. | |
| **Climate** | Temperate, with two rainy seasons (February to April, November to January) | |
| **Population** | Approx. 12.2–12.3 million | Highest population density on the continent |
| **Age Structure** | 0–14 years 41.38%; 15–24 years 19.34%; 25–54 years 32.77%; 55–64 years 4.09%; 65 years and older 2.43% (CIA World Factbook 2017 est.) | |
| **GDP** | Nominal GDP: 1.869 billion Rwandan Francs (National Institute of Statistics of Rwanda) | GDP per capita is US $754.10. (2017 IMF est.) |

| Natural Resources | Minerals, crops, methane, coffee, tea, pyrethrum | |
|---|---|---|
| Currency | Rwandan Franc. 854.7 RwF to $1 US; 1,159 RwF to 1 pound (2017) | |
| Language | Four official languages: Kinyarwanda, English, Swahili, French | In 2008 English became the language of instruction in secondary schools (previously French). |
| Religion | Roman Catholic 43.73%; Protestant 49.5%; Muslim 2%; Animist 0.9%; Other 0.9%; None or unspecified: 3.9% (CIA World Factbook 2012 est.) | |
| Government | Republic with an elected president. Executive, Judicial, and Legislative branches | 2003 Constitution amended in 2015 to allow presidents more than two seven-year terms |
| Media | Re Reporters without Borders, rated 159 out of 180: "ubiquitous censorship and self-censorship." Newspapers: *New Times* (in print and online), *KT Press, News of Rwanda* (in English). Kinyarwanda publications incl. *Umuseke, Imvaho Nshya,* and *Muhabura* (also in English). Some French-language channels. Radio Rwanda very popular. Also many private stations. Local TV limited— the Rwanda Broadcasting Corporation broadcasts in Kinyarwanda and English. BBC and some French channels often available. Main satellite TV provider is DStv. | |
| Electricity | 220–240 volts, 50 Hz | |
| TV/Video | DVD/Blu-Ray Region 5; SECAM | |
| Internet Domain | .rw | |
| Telephone | Country code: 250 | |
| Time Zone | GMT +2 (Central African Time Zone) | |

# chapter one

# LAND &
# PEOPLE

## GEOGRAPHY

Rwanda is located in Central-Eastern Africa,
approximately sixty miles south of the Equator.
It is landlocked and bordered by the Democratic
Republic of the Congo (DRC), Burundi, Tanzania,
and Uganda. Though Rwanda's population is over
twelve million, it is one of the smallest countries on
the continent. It is also the most densely populated
country in Africa. According to the World Bank,
Rwanda has a population density of 483 persons
per square kilometer (1,251 per square mile).

Rwanda's topography is influenced by its
presence on the Albertine Rift and the volcanic
Virunga mountain range along the country's
northwestern border. A drive from Gisenyi in the
northwest to Rusumo in the southeast reveals that
the land gradually flattens from steep mountains
to flatter, dryer savannah, with an abundance of
papyrus swamps and marshes along the course of
the Nyabarongo River. This river, itself the source
of the Nile, begins in the northwest and snakes its
way southeast, where it becomes the Kagera. The
Kagera then forms Rwanda's eastern border as it

finds its way back north and toward Uganda, where it empties into Lake Victoria. Historically, Rwanda has been protected by the natural barriers of Lake Kivu in the west, the Virunga Mountains in the northwest, and the Kagera River to the southeast and east. It is largely because of this natural isolation that Rwanda remained a well-guarded political entity for centuries.

Rwanda's nickname is "The Land of a Thousand Hills," or *Igihugu cy'Imisozi Igihumbi* in Kinyarwanda. To traverse Rwanda is to wind around and over endless hills that ripple the countryside. This hilliness has earned Rwanda the second moniker of "The Switzerland of Africa." Though the country is tiny by African standards, a drive from Kigali to the eastern or western border

can take three hours. While the arterials are paved and of good quality, winding roads and strict speed limits make for slower going.

Because Rwanda's population depends heavily on farming, the countryside is a tapestry of geometric plots and terraced hills. A number of national parks offer the visitor variety from the farmland, though, and it is in these parks that you may enjoy a more virgin display of Rwanda's natural beauty. In the north, the Volcanoes National Park offers not only dense, mountainous jungle, but some of the only remaining mountain gorillas in the world. In the southwest, the Nyungwe National Forest offers thick jungle, treks, canopy walks, and a chance to view the chimpanzee. In the east, the vast Akagera National Park plays host to Africa's well-

known savannah animals, including hippopotamus, elephant, giraffe, Cape buffalo, leopard, gazelles, elands, zebra, baboons, colobus monkeys, and a dazzling plethora of birds. Thanks to the concerted efforts of Rwandan conservationists, lions were reintroduced in 2015, and rhinoceros in 2017. Rwanda is now proud to boast all of Africa's "Big Five" mammals: elephant, leopard, Cape buffalo, lion, and rhinoceros.

## CLIMATE

Rwanda's climate is relatively mild in comparison to its neighbors'. According to the CIA World Factbook, the climate is "temperate." What this means in practice is that temperatures at midday can be quite hot, while things cool off quite a bit in the evening.

In the west and mountainous north, the nighttime chill can call for much warmer layers of clothing when the sun goes down. The Bugesera region just south of Kigali, and the flatter, lower regions in the east can be quite hot and dry. More than the heat, however, the dust during the two dry seasons can be quite bothersome, except in the west. In particular, the ruddy dust tends to coat everything in a light reddish-pinkish layer of grime, especially if you find yourself wandering off the road. You can expect a cleaner atmosphere during the two rainy seasons, from February to April, and then from November to January. During the rainy seasons the weather is warm to hot, with several downpours during the day lasting about thirty minutes or so.

## CITIES AND TOWNS
### Kigali

If you are flying in to Rwanda's Grégoire Kayibanda airport, Kigali will be your arrival point. The city is made up of a number of distinct neighborhoods and contains a population of more than one million. Frequently the object of praise for its order and cleanliness, Kigali is dynamic, vibrant, and offers anything the visitor may require. On the one hand, it teems with authentically Rwandan shops, neighborhoods, cafés, and markets. Just stroll down the two parallel streets in the Nyamirambo neighborhood, for example, and you will see dozens of shops that offer clothing, tailoring, electronics, meat, sporting goods, office supplies, hairdressing, groceries, and household goods. Shopping areas like this abound, with hand-painted frescoes and signs beckoning the buyer in. For a more authentic shopping experience for anything from fresh produce to textiles to crafts to tools, you will not only find what you need at the teeming Kimironko Market in the city's northeast, but you will also find a much better price than in town.

On the other hand, Kigali has an ever-growing number of Western-style shopping centers. Several of these are located downtown, with the Union Trade Center (UTC) being the most central. Inside, the Kenyan-owned Nakumatt grocery store offers everything from fresh meat to electronics. The newly opened Kigali Heights complex in Kimihurura sports several trendy restaurants, bars, clothing stores, and bookshops. For an awe-inspiring sample of modern architecture and one

of the city's most notable architectural landmarks, make sure to visit the recently inaugurated Kigali Convention Center, prominently located along the KN5 road leading from the airport. Designed to replicate the Nyanza king's palace of pre-colonial Rwanda, the Convention Center hosts state-of-the-art meeting centers, as well as the Radisson Blu Hotel.

Beyond shopping, Kigali offers a wide range of nightlife options, including several hip nightclubs popular with Rwandans and Westerners. The city regularly hosts music and arts festivals of local, regional, and international performers. For the sports enthusiast, two large stadiums—Amahoro Stadium in Remera, and Nyamirambo Stadium at the southern end of Nyamirambo—offer local and international soccer matches. Kigali also boasts a wide variety of accommodation choices, ranging from the moderately priced guest houses to the upscale offerings of the likes of the Hôtel des Mille Collines (of *Hotel Rwanda* fame), Serena, and the Marriott, to name only three.

Beyond offering amenities of interest to tourists, Kigali is the seat of the Rwandan government, and also houses international embassies, including the American Embassy and the British High Commission. A drive around the Kacyiru neighborhood will take you past many countries' embassies as well as many of Rwanda's ministries, including the Rwandan Parliament. Seated atop a manicured lawn, the Parliament building's western façade bears witness to the civil war and genocide that racked the country in 1994. Still riddled with bullet and rocket holes left in place as a reminder of Rwanda's past, the building stands as a testament not only to the country's bloody history, but also to its promising present and future.

## Other Towns

Though most visitors will spend much of their time in Kigali, Rwanda contains a number of towns that either serve as stopping points for other areas of interest, or are worth visiting in their own right. Before exploring Rwanda, though, keep in mind that the Rwandan government renamed a number of cities in 2006 in an attempt to erase negative associations with their roles in the 1994 genocide. Among Rwandans, you may hear both names used and whether someone uses the old or the new name usually depends upon their age. The pre-2006 name is not taboo or painful, however; rather, you should keep both in mind and opt first for the post-2006 name. Below, the pre-2006 names appear in parentheses.

**Musanze (Ruhengeri):** This attractive town to the north of Kigali features several first stops on your way to gorilla trekking. Unless you stay in one of the more luxurious lodges closer to the Virunga Mountains, you are likely to stay in one of the hotels here, or stop for a bite on your way up. Musanze is also home to Hotel Muhabura, where Diane Fossey stayed in Room 12 during her famous research of the mountain gorilla. You can see her room. On the way from Kigali to Musanze, you can also stop to visit the Sina Gérard factory in Nyaringarama, where the fiery Akabanga pili-pili sauce is made, along with a bottled version of *urwagwa*, Rwanda's banana beer.

**Gisenyi:** This beautiful resort town is nestled on the shores of Lake Kivu in the west, and it is the main port of entry into the DRC. The city boasts a number of good-quality hotels (some with a private beach) that can be a useful first stop for gorilla or volcano trekkers heading into the DRC.

**Huye (Butare):** Located about three hours to the southwest of Kigali, Huye is home to Rwanda's National University, whose library offers valuable books on Rwandan culture, linguistics, and history. Huye is also home to the National Museum of Rwanda. This ethnological museum is dedicated to pre-genocide and pre-colonial Rwanda, and includes a life-size mock-up of the king's traditional

home. The city is also not far from Nyanza (to its north), the former seat of the Rwandan monarchy and home of the King's Palace Museum. Should you wish to visit one of the most horrific memorials of the 1994 genocide, Huye can be a crossroads on your way to Murambi Technical School, where hundreds of mummified bodies of victims massacred in 1994 lie on display in twenty-four empty classrooms of the unfinished school.

## THE PEOPLE

Rwanda is a diverse society—not so much in ethnic or racial categories, but rather in people's personal histories, their relationships and attitudes toward other groups of Rwandans, and their relationship to Rwanda's official languages. Because Rwanda is diverse, it is challenging to speak about "Rwandans" in broad strokes. What one Rwandan finds true, another may not; and everyone's story is different. Many Rwandans may even provide contradictory interpretations about etiquette. So it is a good idea to keep your eyes and ears open, observe how people interact and behave, and imitate what seems appropriate. As the Rwandan proverb goes, *Ugiye iburyasazi, azirya mbisi*, "When you go to where there are flies, eat them raw." In other words, when in Rome, do as the Romans do—but even more so.

In Rwanda there are many distinctions between people—some immediately evident, some more ingrained in Rwandans' consciousness. Probably the most obvious is that between rural and urban, followed by socioeconomic differences. Urban and better-off Rwandans are more likely to speak English or French instead of just Kinyarwanda, and they are more likely to have completed secondary, if not higher, education. Urban dwellers are also likely to have more experience of dealing with foreigners and Western culture in general. This means that many traditional ways of interacting may be giving way to Western forms of behavior, especially among the young. In the provinces, however, your presence as an outsider or *umuzungu* will be noticed more, sometimes vocally, as people—especially children—openly call out to you. Among rural Rwandans, Kinyarwanda and French are more likely to be spoken, with smatterings of English or Swahili. There is more poverty in the provinces, and rural lifestyles tend to be dictated by farming.

Further diversity has resulted from the waves of migrations and repatriations over the past sixty years. In 1959, fearing an uprising by the Hutu majority (see "History," below), thousands of Tutsis fled into Uganda. There, a new generation of Rwandans was born and raised, speaking English, Swahili, and Luganda, with Kinyarwanda being spoken mostly in the family. When these "old caseload" refugees returned to Rwanda following the 1994 genocide, many settled in Kigali and other cities, where they formed a formidable English-speaking population. While the Ugandan-raised Rwandans speak fluent Kinyarwanda, many Rwandans claim that they can tell just by the person's accent where they grew up.

Beyond linguistic differences, a psychological distance exists between Rwandans who were in Rwanda during the genocide and those who were in the diaspora. Both survivors and returnees have felt difficulty relating to each other and truly understanding each other's backgrounds—Rwandans who were in the country during the genocide directly experienced and witnessed unspeakable horrors that those abroad only experienced secondhand or through reports. Added to this mix are the "new caseload" returnees, the roughly two million Rwandans—mostly Hutu—who fled Rwanda in July 1994, into Zaire (now the Democratic Republic of Congo), in fear of the advancing Rwandan Patriotic Army. While many of these refugees were ordinary citizens, many perpetrators of the genocide fled as well, often blending in with innocent Rwandans. Over the years, many of these Rwandans have returned to reintegrate into Rwandan society, thereby constituting yet another layer of diverse personal—and historically burdensome—experiences among Rwandans. While it is patently false that all Hutus were implicated in the genocide, the association remains in the minds of some and can cast a shadow over relations.

### The Charged Question of "Ethnicity"

This brings us to the inevitable topic of "ethnicity" in Rwanda. Anyone even vaguely familiar with Rwandan history—especially twentieth-century

Rwandan history—will have encountered the terms "Hutu," "Tutsi," and, to a lesser extent, "Twa." To a Westerner, these concepts can prove confusing, as exemplified in the films *Sometimes in April*, when a journalist asks, "These rebels [the RPF], are they Tutu or Hutsi?" and in *Hotel Rwanda*, when an American journalist remarks of two women, one Hutu and one Tutsi, "They could be twins." For many Westerners unfamiliar with Rwandan society, "Hutu" and "Tutsi" have racial or ethnic overtones; however, the reality is a much more complex story of socioeconomic castes and former colonizers' manipulating concepts of racial identity.

The terms "Hutu," "Tutsi," and "Twa" are problematic at best, devastating at worst. In the minds of Rwandans, these divisions have existed for centuries, but primarily as socioeconomic distinctions that were then racialized by the Belgian colonizers. Only since the 1994 genocide have they been so categorically challenged by the Rwandan government and Rwandan society. Today, Rwanda's efforts to obliterate "ethnic" divisionism can be seen in the nationwide slogan, *Ndi umunyarwanda*, "I am Rwandan." The idea is that, above all, Rwandans are *not* Tutsi, Hutu, or Twa; they are Rwandan. From a historical standpoint, an attempt to efface these divisions from people's minds is understandable, given that so much suffering has occurred over the years in the name of these labels.

Prior to 1994, Rwandans were taught through racist propaganda that the differences between Tutsi, Hutu, and Twa were primarily ethnic: that the Twa—or "Pygmies" (now considered a derogatory term)—were the indigenous inhabitants of Rwanda's region; that the Hutu were of Bantu origin and migrated into the area long before the Tutsi; and that the Tutsi were of Nilotic origin, migrating south from Ethiopia in the fourteenth century. Along with these "origin myths" came a myriad racial stereotypes claiming that each group held physical characteristics making them physically distinct from each other. As any Rwandan will tell you, however, this notion of "ethnicity" runs counter to other African countries' notions of ethnicity, which are often connected to differences in language, culture, and religion. Since the inception of the Rwandan kingdom in the eleventh century, Rwandans (the *Abanyarwanda*) have spoken one language, Kinyarwanda, and have shared a belief in *Imana*, the benevolent deity. They have also shared many cultural practices. Therefore, are these really "ethnic" groups? Or are they purely social constructs? Or psychological constructs?

Prior to the arrival of the Belgian colonizers, the understanding of Hutu–Tutsi–Twa was mainly socioeconomic: a Tutsi was someone who owned at least ten cows, that is, a pastoralist; whereas a Hutu was an agriculturalist; and a Twa would primarily be concerned with pottery and hunting–gathering. Because cows have traditionally been associated

with wealth and status,
Tutsis, therefore, largely
became associated with
wealth and high status.
Still, these "castes"
were not set in stone;
a Hutu could become
Tutsi, and a Tutsi
could become Hutu.
During the Rwandan
monarchies from the

eleventh to the mid-twentieth centuries, the kings
(*abami*) were Tutsi; and under Belgian colonial
rule, from 1919 to 1962, the Tutsis were elevated
to the status of the elite.

Two other social arrangements also reinforced
the divide between the Hutu and the Tutsi. On the
one hand, there existed for centuries a serf–lord
relationship between Hutu agriculturalists and
Tutsi landowners known as *ubuhake*. Much like
vassal relationships in pre-Revolutionary France,
Hutu peasants cultivated the land and rendered
crops to the Tutsi landowner, who in return would
offer protection and services. On the other, the
division between Tutsis and Hutus was accentuated
under Mwami (King) Kigeri IV Rwabuguri (1840–
95) through the imposition of *uburetwa*, or regular
forced labor, from which Tutsis were exempt.

Rwandans will quickly point out that the
Belgian colonizers did much to enflame Hutu–
Tutsi relations. Operating within the racial

ideologies prevalent in 1930s Europe, the Belgians actually began classifying Rwandans by physical characteristics, measuring noses, eyes, skull dimensions, and height. In 1933, ethnicity appeared on Rwandan identity cards, "officially" marking the bearer as Hutu, Tutsi, Twa, or Naturalized. These ethnic identity cards were banned only in 1994, after the genocide and the devastating effects they had on their bearers. The Hutus—constituting about 85 percent of the Rwandan population—suffered under the preferential treatment given the Tutsi. Resentment grew until the late 1950s, when the Belgians quickly switched preferences. This, along with other growing tensions between Hutus and Tutsis, led to an uprising by the Hutu, who, not unlike the Third Estate in the French Revolution, reacted violently against the Tutsi. Many were killed, Tutsi homes were destroyed, and many thousands of Tutsi fled the country, establishing a diaspora population, primarily in Uganda. It was these refugees' insistent desire to return to Rwanda during the second half of the twentieth century that led to increasing intergroup tensions in Rwanda. Periodic anti-Tutsi pogroms flared, with tensions spiking in 1990, when the largely Tutsi Rwandan Patriotic Army (RPA) invaded Rwanda from Uganda. Though the RPA was driven back by the Rwandan army (which was supported by French troops), tensions within Rwanda exploded in 1994 with a genocide that cost one million people their lives.

In Rwanda today, evidence of Hutu–Tutsi–Twa thinking still exists, though this never emerges publicly. The social and psychological distinctions between Hutu, Tutsi, and Twa have existed in Rwandans' minds for centuries, and old habits die hard. Still, strict anti-divisionism and anti-genocide ideology laws criminalize distinguishing others based on "ethnic" lines. This is understandable, given that millions of Rwandans

still live with the visceral memory of a genocide in which people were targeted because of their "ethnic" label, as well as decades of persecution and second-class treatment prior to 1994.

Despite any traces of Hutu–Tutsi–Twa thinking that may remain in Rwandan minds, the visitor should avoid thinking in terms of these labels. For one, they have been the source of conflict for many, many years. By definition, suggesting that one person is Hutu and another Tutsi divides people. Always remember that in Rwanda, it is *highly* inappropriate and taboo to ask someone about their "ethnicity," directly or indirectly. This is deeply personal and even political. Moreover, it implies conflict, as a Rwandan's identifying themselves as Hutu, Tutsi, or Twa will evoke a charged history that could suggest victim or perpetrator status, socioeconomic status, or even perceived intelligence. If you ask a Rwandan about their "ethnicity," they may also suspect that you are seeking to determine if they are a victim or perpetrator, two assumptions that are both unsuitable and inaccurate. Also, to think of Rwanda in terms of "ethnic" groups is to remain anchored in the past. Rwanda has made astonishing strides in the years since 1994 in all areas of society; it is a forward-thinking nation. To label Rwandans as Hutu, Tutsi, or Twa is, in many ways, to ensure that the specter of conflict never fades.

## A BRIEF HISTORY
### Clan Allegiances and Monarchy

Prior to the establishment of the Rwandan monarchy in the eleventh century, the area known today as Rwanda was populated by groups affiliated by clan or lineage. Clans were more or less extended family structures, with alliances forming through marriage. Of these approximately twenty clans, the most powerful and populous became the Abanyiginga clan, from whom most of the kings would later emerge.

The first king of Rwanda was Gihanga Ngomijana. Gihanga ruled during the eleventh century in the current Gasabo region in the southeast. Since their beginning, Rwanda's kings were seen as ruling by divine right, with the creator, *Imana*, investing them with power. The *mwami's* (king's) will was God's will, so much so that the king was also referred to as *Nyagasani*, or "Lord." Aside from the king, the Queen Mother held great influence at court, as did the *abiru*, a group of royal advisors. The monarchy's power was symbolized by the royal drum, *kalinga*, and the military played an essential role in the defense and enlargement of the kingdom. When monarchs defeated or annexed other territories, the power loss was symbolized by the stealing of the losing clan's drum. Over the centuries that followed, Rwanda's kings regularly sought to expand the kingdom through conquest, giving rise to a new proverb: *U Rwanda ruratera ntiruterwa*, "Rwanda attacks; it is not attacked."

Kigeri IV Rwabugiri (1853–95) was perhaps Rwanda's most powerful monarch. He readily invaded and annexed neighboring territories, expanding Rwanda's territory to close to its current borders. After his reign, however, intrigue and

infighting greatly weakened the monarchy, which was brought to its knees in 1896 by a bloody interclan coup over royal succession. Known as the Coup d'état of Rucunshu, this crisis, along with other unrest elsewhere in the monarchy, was the context in which Germany

took colonial control of Rwanda–Urundi at the 1885 Conference of Berlin, though Germany did not actually establish an administrative presence in current Rwanda until 1899.

Further disputes in the kingdom continued to weaken the monarchy in the coming years. In the end, Rwabugiri would not be Rwanda's last monarch, but never again would the Rwandan monarchy be as powerful as it was prior to the Europeans' arrival. Especially under Belgian rule, the monarchy, if anything, remained largely symbolic, until Rwanda's

last king, Kigeli V Ndahindurwa, fled Rwanda in
1961, after a parliamentary referendum brought
Rwanda's centuries-old monarchy to an end. He
died in 2016 in exile in the United States.

### The Trying Twentieth Century: a Powder Keg of Intergroup Tension

After Germany's defeat in the First World War,
administrative control of Ruanda–Urundi was
"given" to Belgium as part of German reparations
for the war. While in Rwanda, Belgian colonizers
may have brought certain administrative,
educational, and agricultural developments,
but they also racialized and inflamed Rwandan

social divisions, leaving a legacy of intergroup
hatreds and suspicion. These animosities exploded
in the 1959 "Hutu Revolution," during which Hutus
revolted *en masse* against the Tutsi in a wave of
pogroms and attacks, sending Tutsis into exile.

After 1959 and Rwanda's subsequent
independence from Belgium in 1962, the monarchy

was abolished and replaced by the Hutu president Grégoire Kayibanda, who led an all-Hutu government under the banner of the Parmehutu political party (Parti du Mouvement de l'Émancipation du Peuple Hutu—The Hutu Emancipation Movement Party). Following the 1959 "Hutu Revolution" and Kayibanda's ascendancy in 1962, intergroup tensions became a constant in Rwanda throughout the next three decades, with sporadic anti-Tutsi pogroms terrorizing the Tutsi population still in Rwanda.

Then, in 1990, the mostly Tutsi-led Rwandan Patriotic Army (RPA) invaded from Uganda, where exiled Rwandans had trained and formed a rebel army in 1987. Their goal: to allow Rwandan refugees to come home and to create a democratic society within Rwanda—which, under President Juvénal Habyarimana (who became president in 1973 after a coup), had become a one-party state favoring the Hutu. The rebels were quickly

pushed back by French and Rwandan forces, but the RPA regrouped in the Virunga Mountains in the north to retrain and recover.

Inside Rwanda, the invasion led to a further spike in anti-Tutsi persecution. Suspicion and paranoia abounded, and hate radio such as RTLM and openly anti-Tutsi/pro-Hutu publications such as the magazine *Kangura* entered circulation. The Tutsi within Rwanda were now seen as "accomplices" (*ibyitso*) to the RPF (the political arm of the RPA), which was rumored to be planning to enter Rwanda and kill or subjugate Hutus. Rwanda had become a powder keg of hate and fear.

Facing international pressure to open Rwandan politics up to the RPF and the exiled diaspora, President Habyarimana signed a power-sharing agreement in the fall of 1993 in Arusha, Tanzania. Known as the Arusha Accords, the agreement paved the way for inclusion of the RPF into Rwanda's government. While the Arusha Accords signaled cross-party and cross-ethnic cooperation, it incensed hardline members of Habyarimana's own party, the MRND (Mouvement Révolutionnaire National pour le Développement). Indeed, Hutu hardliners wanted nothing to do with the RPF and the Tutsi, and they saw Habyarimana as being too soft.

### The 1994 Genocide of the Tutsi

On the evening of April 6, 1994, Habyarimana was returning to Rwanda from Dar es Salaam in his private jet, along with Burundi's president, Cyprien Ntaryamira. As the plane approached Kigali airport, it was struck at approximately 8:30 p.m. by two surface-to-air missiles from Kanombe, a military base just east of the runway. The plane exploded, killing all on board and sending wreckage into the President's own backyard, where it can still be viewed today. To date, we still do not know for certain who assassinated Habyarimana. Was it Hutu extremists trying to eliminate him so that they could pursue their anti-Tutsi agenda? Was it the RPF, hoping to reignite the 1990 civil war and take Kigali? Was it Belgian mercenaries? Theories supporting each of these hypotheses have been advanced over the years, but to date no smoking gun has been discovered. An investigation into the assassination by French courts was even reopened in late 2016, closing only in December 2017. At the time of the writing of this guide, the results of this probe have not been made public.

Almost immediately upon the President's assassination, roadblocks appeared throughout Kigali and murders of political moderates and the Tutsi elite began. These murders targeted Hutu moderates as well, including the Hutu Prime Minister, Agathe Uwilingiyimana, who was murdered on April 7, 1994. Soon the Interahamwe—an extremist youth militia affiliated with the MRND—joined in the fray. Ordinary Tutsi were targeted, and it wasn't long before all Hutu were being called by RTLM radio and government officials to "go to work," "clear the bush," and "cut down the tall trees"—codes for killing Tutsi. The killings spread from Kigali to the provinces, and they occurred in the most brutal manner: face-to-face with machetes, clubs, hoes, spears, and sickles. Over the next hundred days, nearly a million Rwandans would perish at the hands of their countrymen.

Almost immediately after Habyarimana's death, the RPF resumed hostilities and began its sweep toward Kigali. While the international community dawdled, the RPA moved quickly toward the capital. Their advance triggered a massive exodus as two million Hutu—terrified of the advancing RPA—fled into Zaire and descended on Goma, a large town just across the Rwandan border. For their part, the French undertook "Opération Turquoise" in June, sending a group of troops into the southwest corner of the country, ostensibly as a humanitarian and protection force. Still, some have indicated that their presence ultimately did little to stop the bulk of massacres, and may have actually offered protection to *génocidaires* who were fleeing westward. After all was said and done, the only group who collectively did anything to actively stop the genocide was the RPF, who took Kigali July 4, 1994, bringing the genocide to an end.

### Post-Genocide Rwanda

With Rwanda in ruins, the RPF took control and set to work rebuilding the country. A transitional government was formed with Pasteur Bizimungu,

a Hutu, at its head. A Government of National
Unity was created, consisting of political parties
that had not been involved in the genocide.
Refugees from the diaspora returned, and,
over the coming years, Rwanda rebuilt itself
bit by bit. The government went about trying
genocide suspects, and the International Criminal
Tribunal for Rwanda was established in 1994 in
Arusha, Tanzania, to try high-level organizers.
To help process the massive number of cases, the
government reinstated *gaçaça*, a "home-grown,"
traditional form of restorative justice whereby
suspects were tried in their communities, as
opposed to in the national courts. This helped
Rwanda to process the overwhelming number
of cases that were clogging the judicial system.
More than this, the Rwandan government has
made a concerted effort to foster forgiveness
and reconciliation among its people, instituting
programs such as *ingando* solidarity camps,

*itorero ry'igihugo* "cultural schools" designed to teach common Rwandan values and history, and the creation in 1999 of the National Unity and Reconciliation Commission, which is still active.

In 2000, President Bizimungu resigned, and the RPF's Paul Kagame stepped into the role. In 2003, the government drafted its new constitution, which remains in force today. Rwanda also held its first post-genocide presidential elections that year; Paul Kagame won with 95 percent of the vote, and was reelected in 2010 and 2017.

Since 2003, Rwanda's recovery has frequently been the source of international plaudits. It has not only rebuilt its infrastructure, but has become an economic power in the region. According to Rwanda's *Economic Development and Poverty Reduction Strategy II* (*EDPRS II*), Rwanda boasted the world's tenth-fastest growing economy from 2000 to 2009. The tourism industry has slowly been growing, and Rwanda has sought to make itself an ICT hub for the region. Students' completion rates of the nine-year basic education program have increased, and—per the *EDPRS II*—Rwanda's GDP per capita growth was 5.2 percent from 2008 to 2012, and the industrial sector grew on average 9.8 percent per year during the same time period. The service sector has also grown remarkably. Beyond mere economic indicators, Rwanda has worked tirelessly to promote unity and reconciliation among its citizens, with the slogan *Ndi umunyarwanda* ("I am a Rwandan") replacing former institutional divisions between Hutu, Tutsi, and Twa.

Rwanda's history remains rich and multifaceted. But of all the historical events, understanding the genocide is vital to an understanding of contemporary Rwanda. The Preamble of the Rwandan Constitution indeed opens by recognizing Rwanda's existence "in the wake of the genocide." Most people over the age of about thirty in Rwanda today have a direct memory of the genocide. And, since 60,000 genocide perpetrators were released from prison from 2003 to 2007, many of the actors in the genocide now live alongside their victims. Many Rwandans have physical and mental scars that serve as constant reminders of past suffering. Atop a prominent hill in the Kimihurura neighborhood of Kigali, the scarred façade of the parliament building looms over the city, reminding all of what happened here just over two decades ago. Memories of the genocide influence education, social programs, and even elections. Rwanda has done much to move beyond the memory of the genocide, but the fact remains that the visitor cannot grasp Rwanda's social and economic efforts, business and work climate, and societal dynamic without understanding the suffering the Rwandan people endured. Rwanda may have been reborn, but Rwandans will never forget.

## GOVERNMENT AND POLITICS

Rwanda is a presidential republic, consisting of an elected president, a cabinet, and elected representatives in a Parliament, itself consisting of the Chamber of Deputies and the Senate. The current Constitution was drafted in 2003 and amended in 2015 to shorten the term limit from seven to five years; the amendment also opened the way for President Paul Kagame to run for a third term in 2017 and then potentially to stand for two more five-year terms. All told, he could possibly remain in office until 2034, serving almost three and a half decades as president.

Officially, Rwanda's government consists of several parties, some of the main ones being the Rwandan Patriotic Front (RPF, or, per its French name, Front Patriotique Rwandais, or FPR), the Democratic Green Party of Rwanda; the Liberal Party or Parti Libéral (PL); the Social Democratic Party, or Parti Social Démocrate

(PSD); and the Centrist Democratic Party, or Parti Démocrate Centriste (PDC). Communication and implementation of government policies operate through a hierarchy of government leaders at every administrative division of Rwandan society.

This is in line with the government's policy of decentralization, according to which local leaders are afforded more responsibility in supporting the government's policies. At the top, there is the nation, Repubulika y'u Rwanda (*igihugu*), followed by the five provinces (*intara*): Kigali City, Northern Province, Eastern Province, Western Province, and Southern Province. The provinces in turn are divided into districts (*akarere*), sectors (*imirenge*), cells (*akagari*), and, finally, neighborhoods (*imidugudu; umudugudu* in the singular). Government directives typically pass down the chain of communication to the *umudugudu,* whose leaders ensure that its members remain informed.

Beyond the Constitution, which provides the legal framework, the government's development decisions are guided largely by two principal documents: *Vision 2020* and the *Economic Development and Poverty Reduction Strategy II* (*EDPRS II*), both of which are available on the Ministry of Finance and Economic Planning Web site: www.minecofin.gov.rw. Much like a company's vision statement, *Vision 2020* lays out six "pillars" of development, while the *EDPRS II* lays out strategies for meeting many of Rwanda's long-term poverty reduction goals (currently, *Vision 2050* and the *EDPRS III* are in the works). To achieve the goals set forth in these, government officials must commit each year to performance contracts (*imihigo*) between themselves and the president. There is strict accountability on officials' meeting their contracts, and their results must be quantifiable. Because such importance is placed on the *imihigo*, any decision that officials make is likely to be affected by the degree to which the decision helps them to fulfill their performance contract and, therefore, bring the country closer to achieving *Vision 2020* and implementing the *EDPRS*.

## THE ECONOMY

Rwanda's main exports are tea, coffee, and minerals. The country's tourism industry is also growing, but Rwanda faces the challenge of competing with regional neighbors whose

tourism industries were not devastated as Rwanda's was by the 1994 genocide. To compete, Rwanda has chosen to emphasize high-end, low-volume ecotourism that caters to visitors seeking a luxury experience such as visiting the mountain gorillas, Nyungwe Rainforest, or Akagera National Park.

Despite increasing tourism revenues, Rwanda's main economic focus has been to develop itself as a knowledge-based economy, paying special attention to becoming an ICT hub for eastern Africa. Rwanda has worked hard to streamline the process of creating businesses and welcoming investors. According to the Rwanda Development Board (RDB), the country currently ranks in the top three African countries in ease of doing business. Using the RDB's online business registration portal, you can even complete the main paperwork for registering a new business in just a day. With the construction of a new international airport in the Bugesera district that began in 2017, Rwanda hopes to increase the volume and ease of travel to the country.

# VALUES & ATTITUDES

A popular slogan in Rwanda is *Ndi umunyarwanda*, "I am Rwandan." Rwandans place great value on their commonalities: their language, their culture, and their traditional beliefs. Accenting commonalities does much to erode divisions that have existed for centuries, and Rwandans are quick to point out their unity and the strength of their culture.

But what does it mean to be Rwandan? For the visitor, certain characteristics may be more noticeable than others—characteristics that Rwandans themselves may not readily notice. This does not mean that these characteristics "define" Rwandans or Rwandanness, but being aware of some of them should help you to navigate a unique and rewarding culture.

## RESERVE AND INDIRECT COMMUNICATION

One of the first characteristics the visitor will notice is that, compared to many Western cultures, Rwandans generally come across as highly reserved—in body language, in friendships, in relationships, in sharing opinions, and in expressing emotions. Even among other Africans, Rwandans can be seen as much more reserved and quieter than their neighbors. You should not be surprised to note that Rwandans you encounter in public will speak softly and, at times, almost inaudibly by Western standards. Among themselves in public, Rwandans tend to speak just loudly enough—so that only their interlocutor can hear what they are saying. There is a great deal of importance placed on being discreet and on others' not knowing your business. Among friends, however, and in private, Rwandans are quick to laugh and have a good time.

Rwandans' reserve also appears in their reticence to show emotions openly. The only emotion that is acceptable to show in public is, generally speaking, mirth. Other emotions—especially negative ones such as anger, frustration, or sorrow—are suppressed or reserved for private spheres. It would be shocking for someone to give vent to anger in public. If this were to happen, other Rwandans present would probably become uncomfortable and skirt the issue by talking about something else and not addressing the contentious point. This emotional reserve can also be seen in everyday interactions, as Rwandans typically show much less emotion in discussions than do Westerners.

One characteristic of the Rwandans' reserved communication style is that of "indirect" communication. Whereas in the West there is pressure to "get to the point" and "say what you mean," in Rwanda discussions usually wander through peregrinations about one's family, the weather, one's impressions of the country, the harvest, sports, or any number of unrelated small topics before finally getting to the real topic of the discussion. Even then, the actual subject may only be hinted at. Imagine, for example, a friend who needs money for a trip to Gisenyi. He may chat about a hundred different topics with his friend, and only mention, subtly and in passing, that the trip to Gisenyi costs 2,000 francs. It is then the listener's job to understand that a request for money has just been made. But rather than offer the money outright, a verbal dance begins in which a suggestion to help is made, the suggestion is refused, and only after one or two more back-and-forths will the person finally accept the offer. In the case of more sensitive topics, Rwandans may talk around the topic or avoid it altogether. It is unusual to hear a Rwandan pronounce a strong opinion on a contentious issue. As some have noted, they may offer a general statement of principle instead, rather than state their personal opinion outright.

In his autobiography *An Ordinary Man*, Paul Rusesabagina (whose story is featured in the 2004 film *Hotel Rwanda*) comments on this communication style, especially in terms of the Rwandans' reluctance to say no. According to Rusesabagina, Rwandans will never tell you "no" outright; rather, they will mention the myriad difficulties that they may face that challenge the fulfillment of your request; they may change the subject altogether, or even lie. Rusesabagina refers to this as the "Rwandan no"—a code that the listener must be attuned to and must decipher in order to understand the point.

### Never Say No

In my own experience, I have never heard a Rwandan directly refuse a request. Either they have said "yes" immediately, or, rather than say "no," they have accepted and then found that something has come up beyond their control. In general, Rwandans are extremely accommodating, and never want to say no—which means that they will simply find something else to say that isn't a direct refusal. I have now learned that, when I suspect the answer to my request will not be yes, I must reassess whether my request is in line with the person's priorities, if they are even in a position to say yes, to reevaluate the request, or to take time to cultivate the relationship before proceeding.

## TRUST

Rwandan relationships are based on trust. If the person doesn't know you, why should they trust you? Are you in Rwanda for personal reasons, or do you sincerely care about Rwanda? Were you introduced by a mutual—trusted—acquaintance? Where are you from? Or, if you are Rwandan, what is your background? What region are you from? Whom do you know? What clan are you from? Or, at an unspoken level, are you Hutu, Tutsi, or Twa?

Rwandans typically have a few small groups of people whom they fully trust. Just because someone is a family member does not automatically mean that they will be trusted—this depends on their past relationship and behavior. In the villages especially, it is not unheard of for Rwandans to hold some of their neighbors in mistrust. This has a historical basis: for almost the entirety of the twentieth century, Rwanda was a society gnawed from the inside by persecution, fear, and mistrust. Prior to 1959, Hutus were largely second-class citizens; and from 1959 to 1994 Tutsis were the target of constant persecution. From 2003 to 2007, this mistrust received a new impetus with the presidential release of more than 60,000 genocide perpetrators from prison. For the most part, these former prisoners returned to their original areas to live alongside their former victims. While much work has occurred to foster reconciliation and renewed trust, suspicion remains in the hearts of many, especially in the older generations.

This mistrust has also been directed outward. Beyond Rwanda's negative experience of its colonizers, Rwandans' experience of the outside world—especially the West—has more recently been scarred by the West's abandonment of Rwanda during the 1994 genocide. Then, the West all but left Rwanda to its fate, which was to lose a million of its citizens in a conflict that destabilized the entire region. Since then, any lingering suspicion of outsiders has shifted. More recently, Rwandans have occasionally expressed frustration at what they see as foreigners' attempts to dictate to Rwanda how to run itself or how to allocate resources—in other words, at attempting to impose Western values on Rwanda without truly understanding its historical and cultural context. Indeed, one common retort to international concerns about Rwandan governance is that Westerners do not fully understand the country's unique situation.

This, however, does not mean that Rwandans automatically mistrust Westerners, for this is not the case. Nor are Rwandans defined by mistrust, and any suspicion that may exist is largely dependent upon an individual's personal situation. What the visitor must appreciate is the high importance of trust in a society that has experienced profound causes for mistrust. As an outsider, you are starting with a handicap, as you have no established background or network within Rwanda. One inroad into building trust is knowing a Rwandan who can introduce you to others. This does not mean that you will gain trust immediately, but you are one step closer.

When developing relationships always seek to build trust over time, and avoid any behavior that may cause others to shy away from you. In negotiations, make sure to emphasize that you are interested in mutually beneficial outcomes, and that you are thinking about Rwandans' authentic needs (and not, say, needs "determined" by a foreign NGO or business).

Never engage in gossip, for to do so could make you appear less than trustworthy. As a recent op-ed by Moses Kirui in Rwanda's leading newspaper *The New Times* advised, gossips "lose all their credibility [. . . ] and people will no longer trust you. They'll wonder what you're saying about them to other people." Indeed, gossip can cause your Rwandan counterparts to shut down and become much more reserved concerning what they choose to share with you.

Trust affects developing friendships. Many long-term visitors to Rwanda claim that it is challenging to make long-lasting friendships. While this is discussed further below, one potential cause of this is the lack of Rwandans' fully trusting the visitor because they may perceive that you are in Rwanda for only a limited time, and that you will probably soon leave.

To counter this, you should make an effort to demonstrate that you are interested in forming long-lasting, non-self-serving relationships. Try to spend time with Rwandans outside work. Send them e-mails or communications from time to time just to say hello. And make an effort to learn some Kinyarwanda, to show your genuine interest in the culture.

## PERSONAL PRIDE AND SAVING FACE

Rwandans have a strong sense of personal pride. Compared to many Western cultures, they place a great deal of importance on maintaining face and being seen as "serious" (*sérieux* in French). To maintain face means to appear in control and calm at all times and avoid conflict; it also means to appear put-together and smartly presented to the outside world. The latter is achieved through dress and behavior—one should be well dressed, and one should behave in a way that maintains discretion and upholds cultural norms.

Understanding Rwandans' desire to preserve face goes a long way to understanding their interaction styles. For example, visitors might initially become frustrated at what appears to be ambivalence toward communication, in that e-mails or direct requests might go unanswered, or be addressed only tangentially. If this happens, be aware that Rwandans are not trying to be evasive or non-committal. Rather, a Rwandan may seem—to a Westerner—to prevaricate not out of disdain or a sudden cold shoulder, but because the person either feels uncomfortable expressing themselves in English, or something else has come up, or you have put a challenging question or request to them that they either cannot fulfill or do not know the answer to. Any of these situations could cause a loss of face. Therefore, avoiding the question or providing roundabout answers can offer a means for preserving face.

In a similar vein, others have drawn attention to the Rwandans' high degree of conflict avoidance. Many in Rwanda will prefer to suppress a disagreement rather than confront someone. You will indeed notice that Rwandans rarely directly focus on a confrontation or difficult question; they are more likely to avoid the awkward topic altogether or only address it in a roundabout way. Sometimes when Westerners present contentious issues to Rwandans directly, they come away wondering if the Rwandans even heard the points. This is because, from the Westerners' perspective, the Rwandans didn't acknowledge what was being brought up. In fact the Rwandans will have understood the issue perfectly, but addressing the challenge directly would have created an awkward discussion, one that could compromise face. A better approach to the situation would be to speak with the other person's interests and point of view in mind, and to soften up difficult topics in a friendly, non-challenging manner that openly shows respect for and even deference to one's Rwandan counterparts.

The importance of preserving face also plays a role in the manner in which Rwandans approach personal mistakes and disagreements. In line with their indirect style of communication, it is unusual to hear Rwandans openly admit to making a mistake; to do so would cause a loss of face. When a mistake is made, they may mention it indirectly, or indicate how factors beyond the person's control may be at play. One of the worst things you could do in Rwanda would be to blame someone directly for making a mistake. While such a blunt approach may work in the West, it will not work in Rwanda; it would be confrontational, and could cause a person to lose face. If this happens, the assumption may be made that you are rude or not "serious," and any future approaches may run into dead-ends.

When interacting with Rwandans, always respect the need to save face and, if you feel that you must bring up a challenging topic or a mistake that has occurred, do so in a friendly, non-confrontational manner, being sure to lace your request with ample apologies.

## GENDER ROLES

The Rwandan government and individual Rwandans are quick to tout Rwanda as being a society of gender equality. The Rwandan parliament indeed leads the world in the number of women representatives, with the legislative body being comprised of 61.3 percent women—a higher percentage than in any governing body in the world. *Vision 2020* also cites gender equality as one of the Cross-Cutting Issues of importance; and policies favoring gender equality feature prominently in both *Vision 2020* and the *Economic Development and Poverty Reduction Strategy II*. Officially, then, Rwanda embraces equality between men and women.

In practice, however, gender equality is still developing, as men and women fulfill very different roles in society. In after-work and leisure time, women are more likely to go straight home to prepare dinner and care for the children, while men may go to a bar for drinks with their male friends. Especially in the provinces, there is a great deal of social pressure placed on women to stay at home after work. Women do not generally attend sporting events, and only women will typically cook, sweep, weed, and carry young children. It would also be shocking for a woman—especially in the villages—to ride a bicycle, climb a tree, drink alcohol, go to a bar alone, or eat goat meat (a Rwandan superstition states that a woman who eats goat will grow a beard). Men typically undertake physically harder work, though you will notice an equal number of women to men hoeing in the fields. In the villages especially, a woman showing her knees might also be seen as promiscuous, whereas a man would not suffer such a blow to his reputation. A woman instigating a divorce might be subject to shame and rumors; a man, not as much. Sadly, there also exist many cases of domestic abuse in Rwanda; the government has recognized this and is taking measures to address the problem.

There is, however, a shift occurring in terms of women's rights and equality. Among the younger generations, more and more women are waiting longer to get married; and more and more women are starting and owning businesses. The documentary film *Sweet Dreams* provides two excellent examples of this. On the one hand, the film documents the Huye-based women's drumming group Ngoma Nshya, unique not only in the quality of the drumming ensemble, but also because drumming has traditionally been reserved for men. On the other, the film traces the women's founding and operation of Inzozi Nziza, a successful ice-cream shop, which is still open. The film's main theme is that of Rwandan women's having a stronger voice in society—a strong force that is slowly growing throughout the country.

## ATTITUDES TOWARD LGBTQ

From a legal standpoint, gay and lesbian people in Rwanda have the same rights and protections as other citizens. In practice, however, homosexuality is taboo, and the 2003 Constitution expressly defines marriage as between a man and a woman. Members of the LGBTQ community therefore maintain much more discretion than in Western countries. As an expat living in Rwanda explains, the attitude toward LGBTQ is "Don't ask, don't tell."

While the LGBTQ community still faces many hurdles to acceptance, this may be shifting. At the 2016 Rwanda Cultural Day in San Francisco, President Paul Kagame even stated that LGBT "... hasn't been our problem, and we don't intend to make it a problem [...], we want to have everybody involved, participating. That means [...] being there for each other." A recent article on the Web site *Mashable* ("Tomorrow, they'll accept us," by Heather Dockray and Danielle Villasana) documents recent challenges, but also strides made by the Rwandan government to prevent mistreatment of the LGBTQ community and Rwandan transgender and LGBTQ activists.


## ATTITUDES TOWARD TIME

A major cultural difference that Westerners find challenging is the different attitude toward time. Conversely, Rwandans have noted Western pushiness and inflexibility when it comes to time and deadlines. While many Westerners organize their days and work strictly according to the clock or calendar, the Rwandan attitude allows for a more organic and less "go-go-go" flow of human interaction. A meeting set for 9:00 a.m. may start at 9:00 a.m., or sometime afterward. A meeting that might last fifteen minutes in the West could easily last three or four hours in Rwanda. If it is raining, expect the delays to be even longer or meetings to evaporate altogether; and if Rwandans appear late for their appointment, you may or may not get an explanation. They have arrived, and they are happy to see you. Why be so obsessed about time?

With this in mind, the visitor to Rwanda should always avoid displays of impatience or irritation. The Rwandan way is neither slow nor selfish; it is centered on priorities other than getting to the point directly and being "punctual." Never force a conversation that you feel is dragging. Insistence and impatience are likely to be seen as pushiness and inflexibility; or even worse, as evidence that a visitor thinks they can push Rwandans around just because they are an *umuzungu* (foreigner, white, or lighter-skinned person). Always remember the Rwandan proverb, *Buhoro buhoro ni rwo rugendo*, "Slowly, slowly goes the journey."

Which brings us to a key word: *Kwihangana,* "to be patient." As Odette Nyiramongi stresses in her book *Ikinyarwanda—the Language of Rwanda: Language Guide for Travelers* this quality is essential to having a successful time in Rwanda. When in Rwanda, you must expect that things will take much, much more time than you are used to.

### Time is Relative

Chatting with a Rwandan who had asked about cultural differences between the United States and Rwanda, I mentioned that in the US people can get upset if you are five minutes late for a meeting. She was shocked. She then explained that, in Rwanda, the first priority is to have something to eat; if you have a full stomach, everything else will fall into place in its own time. Why worry about a few minutes?

## ATTITUDES TOWARD WORK

Rwandans are an industrious people who value work. According to the *EDPRS II*, the majority of employed Rwandans work in the services sector, followed by the agricultural sector, and then industry. One challenge faced by Rwanda, however, is a lack of trained personnel. This especially applies to jobs in the knowledge industry—such as ICT—an area in which Rwanda hopes to be a regional leader. A high dropout rate in secondary schools contributes to this, as many Rwandans leave school because of obligations at home or inability to pay school fees. For those who do complete secondary school, it is not uncommon to return to their village to help with family needs. Many barriers prevent the average Rwandan from completing university, which can open doors professionally.

The working day in Rwanda can last from 8:00 or 8:30 a.m. to 5:00 or 5:30 p.m. or later, with one to one and a half hours for lunch. Though some do, people rarely bring work home, choosing to answer e-mails, analyze data, and so on, during working hours. For work, Rwandans dress exceptionally well; they place great value on a clean and well-dressed appearance and being seen as "serious."

For farmers and peasants the working day largely depends on the season and the harvest. Work begins early in the morning, with a period for rest and lunch at midday, the hottest time of day. They naturally wear clothing appropriate to the job.

It is not unheard of in Rwanda for workers not to be paid for stretches of time. Rather than complain, however, they may prefer to do nothing they consider might jeopardize their job, considering that it is better to have a job than not, especially in an economy where good jobs are hard to come by. As one Rwandan explained, if you complain to your superior, you risk not only endangering your job, but also upsetting people connected to your superior, who may have a say in your future employment. As such, he would sooner keep his grievance to himself rather than create what he fears could be a possible conflict. While it may not be true in a literal sense that complaining can jeopardize your job, this explanation again underscores the indirect way of approaching conflict common in Rwanda.

## ATTITUDES TOWARD FOREIGNERS

Rwandans are hospitable and friendly toward foreigners, especially those who show an interest in the country's culture and people. They are quick to be helpful, and they particularly warm to foreigners who have learned some Kinyarwanda and make a sincere effort to communicate in the local language.

The foreigner in Rwanda will no doubt hear the word *umuzungu* during the course of his or her stay. Though the term generally denotes a white person, *umuzungu* is often also used to refer to multiracial persons, or persons whose skin color is lighter than that of a native Rwandan. Perhaps a better definition would be "Western non-Rwandan." However, the word can also denote the rich, or refer to Rwandans thought to be acting like an *umuzungu*. A Rwandan friend recounts that once when he was out jogging other Rwandans shouted "*umuzungu!*" at him, for this was seen as *umuzungu* behavior. Unlike in the West, where racial terms are highly offensive, *umuzungu* is generally not derogatory. Rwandans may use it either simply to note the presence of an *umuzungu*, or to highlight cultural differences between the *umuzungu* way and the Rwandan, or African, way. That said, the etymology of the word is revealing—it derives from the Swahili verb *zunguka*, "to wander around; to spin around on one spot."

While this might suggest the East Africans' original association of *abazungu* with travel, one could also interpret it as meaning that *abazungu* were originally seen as lost or confused.

Other foreigners with a large presence in Rwanda are the Chinese and Indians. Rwandans typically would not use *umuzungu* to refer to persons of Asian origin. Rather, they would refer to the Chinese as *umushinwa* (plural, *abashinwa*), and Indians as *umuhinde* (plural, *abahinde*).

Unfortunately, many Rwandans equate *abazungu* (plural of *umuzungu*) with money. The assumption is often that if a Westerner has enough money to travel to Rwanda, they surely have enough to spare a little for someone who needs food or gas. It is highly common for Rwandans—especially children, or in smaller towns or rural areas—to ask Westerners for money or other material goods. This is not limited to any one age group—children and adults may ask for *amafaranga* ("money"). The most appropriate reply would be *Oya, ntayo mfite. Mbabarira* (OH-yah, NHAY-oh MFEE-tay. MBAH-bah-lee-lah), "No, I don't have any. I'm sorry." The simple fact is that while need does exist, gifts are not the best way to address these needs; even the Rwandan government discourages giving handouts.


## ATTITUDES TOWARD MONEY

Aside from more well-to-do or middle-class families, money is a day-to-day concern for most

Rwandans. As a Rwandan adult, your first priority is to provide for yourself and your family each day. The question that dominates the lives of many is: Do I have enough to eat for today? For most Rwandans money is simply the means of · providing their daily needs, such as food, gas, drinks, or medicine. As one expat explains, for this reason it is more common to see Rwandans purchasing supplies and food as the need arises, rather than putting away reserves for the future.

This does not mean, however, that Rwandans do not put money into savings or invest. Many local cooperatives exist to encourage people to save. In some cases, these cooperatives function without using a bank; instead, they are community-based savings accounts based on some common activity or status such as unemployed women, farmers, or teachers. A group of *moto* taxi drivers may, for example, meet and agree that each member should invest 500 RwF per month (about 60 cents, or 46 pence). Each member is then responsible for paying their dues each month. Should a member need a loan, they may borrow from the fund at a lower interest rate than they would had they been borrowing from a bank.

Among friends, Rwandans may see "loaning" money as more of a gift, with little expectation of repayment, especially for smaller sums. Furthermore, if one person who has loaned another money does wish to get the money back, they will probably go about this indirectly, perhaps hinting at the money in passing.

For the visitor, differing attitudes toward money can lead to cultural misunderstandings. One area where visitors have been caught off-guard is that of invitations. If you ask a Rwandan acquaintance to join you for a drink or meal at a restaurant, it is understood that you will pay the bill. On the other hand, if a Rwandan invites you out to eat or have a drink, you should never order from the more expensive items. Always choose something moderately priced.

Rwanda is still very much an all-cash society, with only a few businesses accepting credit or debit cards. Though you will find ATMs in Kigali, these may or may not recognize your international card. It is, therefore, not unusual for Rwandans to carry cash—sometimes even large amounts by Western standards—as cash is the primary means for payment among individuals. If you are purchasing something that costs less than, say, 3,000 RwF, you may find that merchants may not immediately have change for a 5,000 RwF bill. It is always a good idea either to try to ensure you have the right amount of money, or to ask the merchant if they have change prior to purchasing, "*Mufite echange?*" (moo-FEE-tay ay-SHAH$^N$-zhuh).

# chapter three

# CUSTOMS &
# TRADITIONS

Today's Rwanda is a blend of traditional and modern. Many of Rwanda's customs can be traced back hundreds of years to a time when Rwandan society was dominated by agriculturalists and pastoralists who believed in Imana, the benevolent creator. In that society, cows played an important role in social standing and relationships, and one's family was all-important as a means of support and developing alliances. Today, Rwandans are ever more influenced by technology and Western culture. In the cities especially, young Rwandans tend to have increasingly Western attitudes toward work, social interaction, money, and technology. It is not uncommon to hear older Rwandans bemoan the younger generation's decreasing familiarity with the "old ways," but tradition still infuses every element of Rwandan culture.

## TRADITIONAL BELIEFS

Before the arrival of Europeans, Rwandans possessed a deeply rooted belief system. This was centered on Imana, the creator of everything, who was benevolent and omnipotent. Rwanda was a place favored by Imana, who, according to the Kinyarwanda proverb, wandered the Earth during the day but came to Rwanda at night to rest: *Imana yilirwa ahandi igataha i Rwanda.*

Unlike the Old Testament or ancient Greek gods who actively meddled in human affairs, Imana left humans and Earthly matters alone. It was the spirits of ancestors, the *abazimu*, that lingered here after death; and the *abazimu* were the ones who interfered in humans' lives. One of the most powerful and revered of the spirits was Ryangombe, a warrior originally from the north, who accomplished many supernatural deeds during his lifetime. When he died, a cult emerged to pray to his spirit for good fortune. Ryangombe's spirit could help in times of misfortune such as drought, sickness, or evil spirits' machinations. Since Imana remained detached from humans, Rwandans would appeal to the spirits of the dead— the *abazimu*, which roamed in places where they used to live—for help in times of need. While one might be tempted to compare the *abazimu* with the saints in Catholicism, the *abazimu* are not truly intermediaries between humans and Imana; rather, they are the only non-material beings in the Rwandan spiritual worldview that directly intervene in human affairs. If the *abazimu* are happy, things are more likely to go well. If they become unhappy, however, hardship can result.

To please the *abazimu*, maintain good fortune, and avoid misfortune, one must go through the *umupfumu*—the Rwandan equivalent of a shaman, or witch doctor. If stricken with a problem or ailment, one would bring one's case to the *umupfumu*, who in exchange for payment might offer talismans, incantations, or a ceremony involving stones, beads, hair, or burning objects to help satisfy the *abazimu*. The *umupfumu* then would also communicate with Ryangombe to solve the problems. Though Christianity and modern medicine have largely supplanted these traditional beliefs, the *abazimu* still hold great sway in the minds of many. In villages especially, people may still know an *umupfumu*, who may be consulted if problems are not resolved.

Today, Rwanda is a highly religious country, with the vast majority of people practicing some

form of Christianity, followed by Islam. In your interactions with Rwandans, do not be surprised to receive blessings and references to God (the Christian God is also called Imana), even in official correspondence. Rwandans may assume that you are Christian without asking. Depending on the people you associate with, you may even be invited to church. Receiving such an invitation is an honor and, even though your personal beliefs may be different, attending Mass or a church ceremony in Rwanda is truly a moving event that should be appreciated for its own merit.

## PUBLIC HOLIDAYS

Aside from religious and historical holidays, the most significant Rwandan holiday is Kwibuka ("to remember"), the week of remembrance commemorating the 1994 Genocide of the Tutsi that begins each year on April 7. During this week, expect things to be much more subdued and somber than normal. Gospel programs will dominate TV broadcasts, and Rwandans themselves may become more withdrawn. This is a time for remembrance and introspection; it is not a time for boisterous activity.

Although it is not technically a holiday, the last Friday of every month is reserved for *umuganda*—mandatory community service for Rwandans. This lasts from early morning until about

11:00 a.m., and the country—that is, stores, restaurants, offices, and services—basically shuts down during these hours, as people contribute their services. If you are driving on the roads at these times you may be stopped by the police. Foreigners are generally exempt from *umuganda*, but Rwandans who are driving on these mornings must have an official exemption note.

### RWANDA'S OFFICIAL HOLIDAYS

| | |
|---|---|
| January 1 | New Year's Day |
| January 2 | |
| February 1 | Heroes' Day |
| March/April | Good Friday (movable) |
| | Easter Monday (movable) |
| April 7 | Genocide Memorial Day. Marks the beginning of Kwibuka, or Memorial Week. |
| May 1 | Labor Day |
| July 1 | Independence Day |
| July 4 | Liberation Day |
| First Friday in August | Umuganura Day (Thanksgiving or National Harvest Day) |
| August 15 | Assumption Day |
| December 25 | Christmas |
| December 26 | Boxing Day |
| Eid El-Fitr and Eid Al-Adha | The Rwanda Muslim Association announces these each year, but usually not until the night before, when the imam sees the Moon. |

## GREETINGS

Whatever the purpose of your meeting or conversation, you should always begin with a proper greeting and a handshake. Ask the person how they are doing, and allow the conversation to wander through small talk before getting to your actual topic. Jumping right in to your topic will be seen as impolite, pushy, and not "serious."

There are three main greetings in Rwanda. Before noon, you will hear *Mwaramutse* (ma-la-MUH-tsay), "Good morning." Between noon and about 5:00 p.m., Rwandans greet with *Mwiriwe* (MEE-lee-way) or (*Muraho* (muh-LAH-ho), "Good day." After about 5:00 p.m., the greeting is *Mwiriwe*, "Good evening." The answer to these is to repeat the greeting, followed by *Amakuru?* (ah-mah-KUH-luh), "How are you?," to which the answer is *Ni meza* (nee MAY-za), "I am fine." Among friends, you will also hear *Bite?* (BEE-tay), "What's up?" Here, the correct answer is *Ni byiza* (nee BYEE-za) "I'm fine."

### Handshakes

When meeting a person for the first time, or when seeing an acquaintance after a separation, it is customary to shake hands with your right hand while looking the person briefly in the eye and offering a greeting: *Muraho. Amakuru?* ("Hello. How are you?"), to which they will respond, *Ni meza. Namwe?* ("I am fine. And you?"). The correct answer to this is always *Ni meza* ("I am fine"). You will notice that, when shaking hands, some people will lightly touch their right forearm with the fingers of their left hand; this is a sign of respect.

It is also common for people to hold handshakes for much longer than in some cultures. You may, for example, meet someone and shake hands. The person will continue to hold on to your hand while they ask about your news or your family. There is no squeezing in this part of the handshake; there is also no shaking. Rather, the handholding allows two people to catch up before continuing on to other things or shaking others' hands. Rwandans may also hold on to your hand as they walk with you or lead you somewhere.

Among (younger) male friends in an informal setting, it is common to greet each other with a quick hand slap and clasp, with both arms held forward and at an angle, as if arm wrestling. This will then be followed by a switch to a handshake, and finished with sliding the hands away while gripping each other's fingers with the tips of your own fingers.

## PHYSICAL CONDUCT

When chatting with someone, do not be surprised if the person stands closer to you than you are used to. Likewise, do not be surprised if the person holds your hand or arm as they speak. Proximity allows for closeness in the conversation, and it allows the two to speak discreetly. If someone steps in close to talk and you step back, the other person may wonder why you stepped back. Are you avoiding them? Is there something about them that you don't like? Standing close and speaking softly, however, help to ensure that trust and confidence are maintained. This will also help others see that you are respectful and "serious."

Though you will regularly see two men or two women holding hands or arms in public, physical displays of romantic affection with your partner or spouse should be reserved for the privacy of home.

Another behavior that is reserved for home (or a restaurant) is eating. While it is common in many Western countries to eat on the street while walking or chatting with friends, eating in public in Rwanda is considered rude. Smoking in public is prohibited.

When you are conversing with a Rwandan, they will acknowledge what you are saying in two ways. First, as you speak or ask a question, they will raise their eyebrows repeatedly, often punctuating this with a soft, "Mmmmm." At the same time, they will lift their head slightly and protrude their lips as if just beginning a pout. For a Rwandan, these gestures communicate that, "I hear you and understand you. I am following you." They may not acknowledge verbally that they are following, but they are. Second, Rwandans often punctuate their conversations with a sometimes short, sometimes long "Eh!" or "Eh?" Depending on the intonation, this can mean a number of things from "Really?" to "You're kidding!" to "I don't believe you," to

"I get it." (One entertaining video online by @Contact_Makeda illustrates quite a few of the different meanings of "Eh"). Rwandans do not generally use demonstrative or animated gestures when in conversation. When they greet you, or as they speak, you will probably notice that they hold a blank, emotionless expression. This largely stems from their natural reserve, as opposed to any sort of emotional distance.

Don't be surprised if you find Rwandans looking you up and down, as if they were examining you head-to-toe. This is much more likely to occur in the provinces, where people are less accustomed to seeing foreigners. This comes mostly from curiosity, as opposed to judgment. In fact, it is common for Rwandans to want to know about your background, which they may assess by looks or, in some cases, through direct questions (for example, *Mutuye hehe?* "Where are you from?"). A person's background plays an important role in interpersonal communications, and even though this may go unspoken, Rwandans are curious to know others' region, clan, or origin as a means of establishing first impressions.

In conversations, it is unusual for people to hold eye contact. Instead, Rwandans tend to look down, or to your side, or beyond you, all the while following what you are saying. Holding direct eye contact is more confrontational.

Finally, one form of communication that you may encounter is hissing. In markets or crowded places, if you hear someone behind you making staccato hissing noises, they are asking you to move out of the way. A Rwandan who sees an acquaintance in public may likewise hiss to get their attention. You may hear Rwandans hissing in restaurants to attract the server's attention. In the better restaurants, however, you beckon with your hand: hold out a flat, downward-facing palm and simultaneously and repeatedly flex the four fingers toward the palm. Westerners have caused confusion by waving in public as Rwandans thought they were being summoned! If you wish to point, point with all four fingers extended, not with your index finger.

## MARRIAGE PRACTICES

Marriage plays an important role in Rwandan culture, with a great deal of pressure being placed on young men and women to marry. At about the age of twenty-five, friends and family may start to ask you your marriage plans. If at thirty you are still single, rumors may spread. If at thirty-five you are not yet married with children, people—especially in the villages—may assume that something is wrong with you.

Traditionally, marriage in Rwanda was not just the union of a man and a woman; it was about forming alliances with other families and clans. Today, marriage is still a marriage to the other person's family. The larger the family, the better the chances—traditionally speaking—of surviving and thriving. With marriage, the groom's or bride's family become your family; and your family will henceforth take an active role in important life decisions.

Weddings in Rwanda are expensive, long-drawn-out affairs requiring much planning. When a couple announces their engagement, friends of the bride and the groom begin calling planning meetings, both to plan the wedding and to secure donations to offset the cost. If you receive an invitation to one of these, you should make a financial contribution. Even in the workplace you may be asked to contribute to a colleague's wedding. Typically, the groom and his family pay for the church service and the reception, whereas the bride's family will pay for the *gusaba* ceremony (see below). During the meetings, organizational roles are also assigned; one person might organize the decorations, another the drinks, another the music, and so on. Regarding refreshments, it is assumed that if a hundred people are invited, three hundred may show up. It is the duty of the groom (in the case of the reception) to make sure that everyone is attended to.

## The Four Ceremonies

There are four main ceremonies, each of which usually take place in different parts of a district or cell: the *gusaba*, the civil ceremony, the church service, and the reception. While this is traditionally the order of the four ceremonies, some couples may change the order.

*Gusaba* usually takes place on a Saturday or Sunday (*gusaba* means "to ask" in Kinyarwanda). In earlier times, there would be much to-do about the groom's asking the bride's family for her hand. This would be a negotiation in which the bride's family would size up the groom and his family, and a dowry—one or more cows— would be agreed upon. In some rural areas, cows may still be offered, but in many places the cow has been replaced by money. Today, *gusaba* is mostly for show. It occurs in a large open tent, with the groom's family and representatives seated on one side, and the bride's on the other. There are music, dancing, decorations, and refreshments. During the ceremony each family—the bride's and the groom's—select representatives to try and "one-up" each other with riddles and banter designed to test each other's (originally, the groom's) worth. Gifts (*ibishingiyanwa*) will also be offered. The bride will pay homage to her future father- and mother-in-law; she will give a hat and a cane to the father-in-law and an *umushanana* (a long skirt with a sash draped over one shoulder) and an *urugori* (wicker tiara) to the mother-in-law. The *urugori* symbolizes the bride's respect for the mother-in-law; it also becomes unacceptable henceforth for the bride to speak any words that constitute the mother-in-law's Kinyarwanda name. Kinyarwanda even includes an alternate set of nouns (known as *gutsinda*) to allow this.

Even if the woman's mother-in-law passes away, *gutsinda* remains in effect as a mark of respect.

Civil ceremonies occur on Thursdays at the district (*umurenge*) level, and the government district leader officiates. Before the civil service, couples must take lessons to learn about finance, marriage laws, and the government's role in marriage. On the day of the service, there may be hundreds of people getting married. Each couple must hold the Rwandan flag and repeat an oath; they then sign marriage certificates, which are also signed by the witnesses, typically close friends of the couple.

The church service follows, on the same or a later day. This ceremony is the most Western of the ceremonies. One difference, however, is that, in Rwanda, the bride is not accompanied by her father. Since the bride was "given" by her father during *gusaba*, the groom brings her from home to the church. As with the civil ceremony, the church also provides lessons on each person's role in the marriage prior to the ceremony.

The culmination of the marriage is the reception, also held in a large tent. As with the *gusaba*, the bride's family sits on one side, and the groom's on the other. The newlyweds occupy the place of honor on two thrones at the front of the tent, with the best man and bridesmaid at their side. Each family selects representatives who take turns paying compliments to the other family, with song and dance punctuating the speeches. There is a wedding cake, which is cut and shared among the guests, and plenty of drinks—alcoholic and non-alcoholic—for all. In some ceremonies, especially where the families particularly venerate Rwandan tradition, the two families may share a bowl of *urwagwa* (homemade banana beer). Receptions typically welcome hundreds of people, and last long into the night.

# chapter four

# MAKING FRIENDS

To an outsider, the Rwandans may at first appear more reserved than their East African neighbors—in speech, in emotions, in body language, and in friendships. However, Rwandans are an entertaining and sincere people who make highly loyal friends, and it is well worth taking the time to cultivate friendships while in the country. Not only will this help to expand your social connections around the world, but it will also bring you closer to appreciating Rwanda and Rwandan culture as an insider.

The Rwandans' natural reserve means that their network of trusted friends may be small, but it is marked by strong loyalty. A great deal of importance is placed on friendship as a means of creating a social support system. Rwandans are highly community-focused, as opposed to individual-focused, as in some Western cultures. The idea that you would make it on your own by "pulling yourself up by your bootstraps" is unheard of in Rwanda. You need friends, and you need family.

For the visitor, making friends with Rwandans may take time, but it is a rewarding experience. Many Rwandans admire Westerners and welcome the opportunity to get to know them better, despite the language barriers and cultural differences. As the Rwandan proverb states, *Ifumbire y'ubucuti ni amagambo,* "Words are the fertilizer of friendship." So when meeting Rwandans, talk, make the effort to get to know them, and you may be rewarded with devoted friends.

## FRIENDSHIP AMONG RWANDANS

Rwandans typically have a small group of trusted friends. These friendships are often formed during school years, in the neighborhood or village when growing up, or at work. Even though their circle of trusted friends may be small, Rwandans often have a larger network of friends than Westerners

do, with the networks constituting different levels of friendship. At the center is the inner circle—those whom you can trust in times of need. These close friends are likely to be ones who will be your witnesses at a civil wedding ceremony; they will also play a role in organizing planning meetings for your wedding. The next level of friends includes those with whom full trust may not yet have been established. They may take a little longer to help out than those in your inner circle. A Rwandan might become suspicious if a friend frequently asks for money or other help, as this could indicate that the "friend" is really looking to gain something, and is not a true friend. As one Rwandan explained, you know a Rwandan is truly your friend when they ask you for nothing.

Friends can also play a role in landing a job. Your friend from school might, for example, know someone who works in, say, a bank, and can introduce you, thus increasing your chances of getting it. Or your friend might have connected acquaintances, which can help you establish trust quickly and be considered. While this does not necessarily mean that you would be chosen over someone more qualified, social networks play an important role in gaining employment. In a word, it's all about whom you know.

The main demands of friendship are loyalty, trust, and helping in times of need. A true friend would never betray secrets or engage in gossip, for these would both constitute violations of trust. As we have seen, Rwandans are highly sensitive about other people knowing their business, and friends play a great role in maintaining confidence.

## MAKING RWANDAN FRIENDS

Westerners in Rwanda sometimes lament that it is difficult to make Rwandan friends. To an extent, this is understandable, given the Rwandans' natural reserve, and that when abroad your natural tendency is to flock to members of your own herd, that is, other foreigners, for cultural and linguistic familiarity. The difficulty in learning Kinyarwanda presents a formidable barrier. Compared to European languages, it is dizzyingly impenetrable due to its dramatic difference from these languages. Add to this the dearth of Kinyarwanda instruction of any quality, and it is easy to give up. Still, making an effort to learn and practice Kinyarwanda is a first step in forming friendships. It is not impossible, and speaking the language—if only a little bit—goes a long way in instilling trust and confidence. This also helps to bridge the Rwandans' reserve, which can be heightened by their unease with speaking English. The truth is, many Rwandans—and Westerners, for that matter—can be intimidated by language barriers and by what they perceive as Westerners being too direct.

As mentioned above, trust is vital. Making a concerted effort to spend time with Rwandans will help to convey that you are interested in sincere friendships. Even though you may be out of your comfort zone, take the trouble to join Rwandans

in their social activities—church, sports, drinks, meals, and so on—and take a sincere interest in getting to know them and their interests. Look for ways to get involved in the community. Even among Rwandans, trust takes a long time to form, and, because you are a foreigner, it will be much harder for you than it would for a Rwandan to establish trust. People may wonder what your intentions in Rwanda are; they may wonder about your motives; or some may even see you as a means to acquire money or material goods. Through persistent effort in showing Rwandans that you are interested in them personally and that you have no ulterior motives, you will build trust.

## LENDING MONEY

At some point in your stay in Rwanda, you will probably be asked for money by all manner of persons: from street children who sidle up to

you and ask *Amafaranga?* ("Money?") to
your Rwandan colleagues and professional
acquaintances. One reason for this is that,
in many Rwandans' minds, an *umuzungu* is
someone who is rich. If asked for money by
someone with whom you have not established
a trusting relationship, always remember the
importance in Rwanda of preserving face. Avoid
an outright no, which could embarrass the other
person. Instead, you may answer with a smile that
you need money, too, and wouldn't life be easier
if things were cheaper? In this way, you indirectly
defuse the request. This also helps to avoid
creating a sense of financial inequality, or a
needs-based relationship, and it preserves face.

## INVITATIONS HOME

It may take a while for enough trust to be built
between you and Rwandans to be invited to
a Rwandan home. If this happens, remember
the Kinyarwanda proverb, *Umushyitsi mwiza
arizimana*, "A good visitor makes himself feel
welcome." What this means is that you should
somehow contribute to the household with a
small gift. If the family has children, you may
bring them Fantas, soda, or candy. If the family
is middle class, you may bring a bowl of fruit or
some wine, or something decorative for their
home. Home-cooked treats are also a good idea.
If you are visiting a more needy family, bring

something that will be of use to the household, such as oil, salt, or rice. No matter what you bring, do not expect your Rwandan hosts to open your gift in front of you. They will save it for later.

Rwandans will always offer someone they've invited home something to drink or, in some cases, to eat. The drink may be milk, soda, or sometimes beer (or, in the villages, *urwagwa*, banana beer), but not water. Milk plays a huge role in Rwandan culture; it is seen as being the purest and most nutritious drink, one that cannot be poisoned, and it is an honor to be offered milk. In the case of bottled drinks, such as beer or soda, you will typically be offered a first drink, which you should accept, but it is not customary to accept a second drink. Your host will typically produce a second bottle and offer it, with his hand hovering over the still-closed bottle cap, but you should politely refuse. If you are offered food, it is rude to refuse, given the high value Rwandans place on having enough food. The only time when it would be acceptable to refuse is if you have a food allergy or religious restriction that would prevent you from eating.

## DATING

Intimate relationships tend to take much longer to develop in Rwanda than in the West. In the West, physical intimacy can come more quickly, but in Rwanda a strong emotional connection must first exist before the relationship becomes romantic. If a Rwandan asks you out to eat or to dance (or vice versa), then the "date" is most likely just that: to eat or dance together as friendly acquaintances. Six months might pass before a couple even considers themselves a couple. Often, a man and a woman will not go out alone together until they have known each other for some time. Or they will at first be together only in a communal setting, such as with a group of friends going out to eat or dance.

Another cultural difference between Rwandans and Westerners is that in Rwanda there is a great deal of pressure on young people to get married. The pressure to be married and have children is especially acute for women, while men feel under pressure to provide materially for a family. As dating relationships form in Rwanda, these are also often kept quieter than they would be in the West. And because public expressions of intimacy are unacceptable in Rwanda, it may be only when they announce their engagement that you become aware that a couple has been dating.

# chapter five

# THE RWANDANS AT HOME

## HOUSING

Rwandan housing varies greatly, depending on the socioeconomic status or location—urban or rural—of the dwellers. In the cities, houses may be made of stucco or brick with tiled roofs; while in the countryside houses are often made of mud brick, stucco, and corrugated metal roofs. In an effort to modernize the country, the government has outlawed thatched-roofed homes. In the countryside, a home (*rugo*) might typically consist of several small buildings clustered together: a

living and sleeping area, a kitchen, and a latrine. The home will be surrounded by a stucco or mud-brick wall or "fences" of planted bushes. Villages form among clusters of homes, which are administratively organized as *imidugudu*. Most villages are accessible by dirt roads that snake off the arterials connecting the larger cities. In the city, houses will also be surrounded by a wall and a (usually) metal door that can be locked. City homes are also organized into *imidugudu*. Middle- and upper-class homes almost always have a night watchman and frequently a houseboy or maid, who takes care of cleaning, laundry, and, sometimes, cooking.

Typically, a house will accommodate a nuclear family, though it is not uncommon for aunts and uncles to live there as well, especially in the countryside. When children come of age to marry, they leave home. Traditionally, Rwandan

men must provide a home as a prerequisite to marriage. This has become increasingly challenging: fewer job opportunities and economic hardship have prevented more and more young men from being able to meet this requirement. In his excellent book *Stuck: Rwandan Youth and the Struggle for Adulthood*, Marc Sommers shows how barriers to marriage have prevented many Rwandan men from being seen as "men" by society. To be seen as a "man" one must be married; but to get married, a man must first be able to provide a house. The result of this is a large group of young men in Rwanda who feel "stuck."

Administratively, Rwanda is highly organized, with governmental communication streamlined from top to bottom. At the smallest level, a group of houses constitute an *umudugudu*. These then form a cell; cells form a sector; and sectors form a district or region. Each *umudugudu* has a leader who is responsible for transmitting governmental announcements to the neighborhood members. This usually happens at the once-monthly *umuganda*, the required community service that takes place on the last Saturday of each month. At the end of the work (around 11:00 a.m.), the *umudugudu* leader makes announcements. The *umudugudu* leader also attends to the neighborhood members' needs or complaints, and works to make sure that they are in compliance with government regulations.

## A SENSE OF STYLE

Rwandans dress well when in public—far better than many casual Westerners, in fact. Women stroll through the cities in bright *kitenge* cloth or smart dresses, while men don neatly pressed slacks and impeccably ironed shirts with polished shoes. The only time you will see shorts in Rwanda will be in a sports setting—say, on people out for a jog or a swim—or on children and adolescents. Rwandans dress quite conservatively; it would be shocking to wear short shorts or a short skirt; likewise, revealing shoulders, knees, midriffs, or cleavage would be inappropriate. While there is something to be said for dressing comfortably and informally, do not expect to be taken seriously in a work setting if you are wearing jeans,

sneakers, and a tee shirt. The visitor should dress well and neatly as a sign both of respect and of the importance of maintaining a polished veneer.

One area in which dressing appropriately is particularly important is when visiting memorials. Appearing at a genocide memorial in shorts, tee shirt, and sandals would be unsuitable and insulting. Of all places in which respect and reverence are called for, none supersede Rwanda's many memorials. Dress conservatively and respectfully, wearing no hats or sunglasses.

Finally, some Rwandans have expressed a bemused frustration at Westerners who show up in Rwanda dressed in safari clothing, as if Africa were one big safari. It is not. It is a continent with thriving and rich cultures, developed urban centers, and sophisticated citizens—much like any other continent. Ask yourself, "How would I dress if visiting Paris, London, or New York?" Dressing for African cities should be no different.

## THE DAILY ROUND

A Rwandan's day usually begins at about 6:00 a.m., when the sun comes up. In the countryside, there

will often be chores such as fetching water, tending to livestock, or cleaning. It is not unusual for children to have to walk long distances to school, in which case they will wake up earlier. After breakfast, the children go to school while the adults go to work—either in an office or in the fields. Both children and adults have at least an hour for lunch. Children typically come home to eat a meal prepared by their

mother. In the city, it is common to see swarms of businesspeople descending on the restaurants, where they will pile their plates high with food from buffets.

After school, children may play together or head home for more chores. If they have been given homework they will need to take care of this quickly, as the light fades rapidly at 6:00 p.m., and more than half the population—mostly in the countryside—do not have electricity. Being able to see one's schoolwork is an issue for many Rwandan children, not to mention the conflicting demands placed on them by chores and schoolwork. It is not uncommon for Rwandan children to have to do chores first, causing schoolwork to suffer. The author has met a number of former schoolchildren in Rwanda who had to stop their studies because domestic responsibilities took priority.

After work, Rwandan women typically go home to prepare dinner and attend to chores, while the men often go for a drink with friends in pubs or *cabarets*, the latter being a type of pub in the countryside consisting of a covered patio area and a somber interior where you can purchase warm beer, peanuts, boiled eggs, *sambusas* (a fried, stuffed, savory pastry), or goat-meat brochettes, a common Rwandan snack.

Grocery shopping is done more frequently than in the West. Rwandans do not typically store food; rather, they buy what they need on a daily basis. In the cities they may do this at the ever-more-common Western-style supermarkets, or at one of the larger, fresh-produce markets. In the countryside, produce will either be produced at home or, if there is some money available, food will be purchased at a market, *isoko*.

## EDUCATION

Primary and secondary education is free in
Rwanda. The grades progress from Primary 1 to
Primary 6 (from seven to twelve years old), and
then from Senior 1 to Senior 6 (from thirteen to
eighteen years old). During primary school (from
Primary 1 to Primary 4), students are instructed
in Kinyarwanda; after Primary 4, the language of
instruction is English. Prior to 2008, all secondary
education was in French. This switch partly
explains why it is more common to encounter
French-speakers among older Rwandans, whereas
younger Rwandans are more likely to speak English.
While there are a few hundred private schools in
Rwanda, there are seven times as many public and
government-assisted schools. At school, students
study a variety of subjects, with languages such as
French and Swahili typically being optional.

Though school is free, many Rwandans face
barriers that prevent them from completing

secondary school. A glance at the Rwandan Ministry of Education's *Education Statistical Yearbook* shows a dramatic drop in enrollment from primary to secondary schools. Many students withdraw or repeat grades for a number of reasons; indeed, the number of students repeating grades can be high. Financially, some families cannot afford various school expenses such as uniforms, materials, or parents' association fees. For others, chores at home or other family situations prevent them from fully engaging themselves. Their grades drop and they either fail the national exam or must withdraw altogether. For other students who do finish secondary school, a life back in the village is often what awaits them, with the family's sustenance or financial pressures precluding the student's ability to attend university.

A student's typical classroom experience will be on a shared bench as the teacher lectures. Most

learning in Rwanda is teacher-centered and by rote: the teacher writes the lesson almost word-for-word on the chalkboard, and the students copy the notes into their notebooks. Students rarely if ever question the teacher. The teacher dispenses knowledge; the students absorb. When the teacher asks an individual student a question, the student may rise to answer. However, there is a sincere desire among educators in Rwanda to move to a less traditional, more student-centered approach that fosters critical thinking. In fact, the new Competence-Based Curriculum (2015) places much more emphasis on student-centered learning, and teacher-training is focusing more and more on shifting the focus from the teacher as authority to the students as agents in their own learning. There is still a ways to go, but teachers are eager to learn and practice new techniques in the classroom.

According to the *2016 Education Statistical Yearbook*, 72 percent of all students enrolled in Rwanda's education system were in primary school (in 2016); only 2 percent were enrolled in universities. Aside from universities, Rwanda also has a number of technical and nursing schools, vocational schools, and adult literacy schools.

# chapter six

# TIME OUT

Rwandans are very friendly, sociable, and quick to laugh and have a good time. They enjoy dancing, music, sports, and good company among friends. While the foreigner might perceive them to be

more reserved than other East Africans, Rwandans enjoy their time out with each other and, if you express a sincere interest in joining in, with guests to their country.

Generally speaking, the way Rwandans spend their free time varies according to their employment status, age, gender, income, and locale (city or countryside). In the provinces, it is not uncommon to see swarms of children milling about after school but before dark (some being quite young), fetching water, collecting grass for goats, watching livestock, collecting wood, or playing soccer or hoop and stick with improvised materials.

A common practice—in the provinces especially—is going to church, with mass being held several days a week and many hours at a time; when not at Mass, rural Rwandans may also go to choir practice for hours on end. These sessions are often audible from quite a distance away, especially if large speakers are involved!

In the cities, Rwandans enjoy having a drink after work with friends, playing and watching sports such as soccer and tennis, hanging out and chatting, listening to music, and (among the younger generation especially) dancing.


## NIGHTLIFE

Kigali and the other cities feature a variety of nightlife options. For those who like music and dancing, Kigali has several popular nightclubs that are popular hangout spots for twenty- and thirty-somethings. If you plan on going to a nightclub, there are several things to remember. First, Rwandans typically go out dancing much later than Westerners; they start at about midnight and stay out until the sun comes up. If you show up at a nightclub at 10:00 p.m., you are likely either to find only other Westerners or a bare dance floor! Second, nightclubs are not the best place for romantic encounters. On the one hand, Rwandans typically take much longer to develop relationships; on the other, it is best—in any country—to avoid making unwise or alcohol-influenced sexual decisions. One common way that HIV is transmitted is through risky sexual behavior while abroad, and it would be wise to be wary of anyone making sexual advances on a first encounter.

For those more interested in a relaxed evening, Kigali has a number of restaurants, wine bars, and distilleries, where you can enjoy a drink and food with friends in a quieter atmosphere.

## EATING OUT

Dining out is typically a middle-class or higher activity. In the cities, this occurs more often at lunchtime, when businesspeople on their break

swarm the buffets that dot the cities. If you go to one of these buffets, diners typically pile their plates high with a mountain of carbohydrates— *matoke* (green bananas), cassava, sweet potatoes, beans, rice, fries, or pasta— with some sort of meat or fish stew on top and cassava greens (*isombe*) or mixed vegetables.

For evening dinners, Rwanda's cities have plenty of options, with the best selection in

Kigali, where you can find traditional Rwandan, Congolese, grilled food, Korean, Indian, Chinese, Italian, German, Ethiopian, and more. The quality of these restaurants is usually excellent. You will also find a wide selection of wines and spirits.

During the day, a popular snack is the goat meat brochette (kebab), usually served with fries. These are readily available throughout Rwanda, in both restaurants and pubs, and are delicious with a cold Mützig or Primus beer and a few drops of the fiery Akabanga sauce (pepper-infused oil). If you are seeking a snack, however, try to avoid street food, as you cannot be sure of the hygiene of its preparation.

## SERVICE

One of Rwanda's goals is development in the service sector. In the better places in Kigali, service personnel take their work seriously, though at times it may be clear that your server is learning the ropes. Regardless of the quality of service, one thing the visitor will notice is that service takes longer than in the West—sometimes significantly longer. Recognizing the imposition that long wait times may pose, some restaurants in Kigali have begun putting approximate wait times on their menus for à la carte ordering. If you decide to order from the menu, be prepared to take your time and enjoy your evening.

If you eat in a pub or café in one of the provinces, you may have to call the server over to be acknowledged. Don't expect him or her to walk over right away, or even acknowledge your presence. A slight hiss and hand wave (which is used to beckon someone) are sufficient.

When shopping in a local market or shop (as opposed to a Western-style store), you may be shadowed by any number from one to four employees. They are not keeping an eye on you to make sure that you don't shoplift—they are following you to be of immediate assistance. At your slightest lingering at an item, they may pull it out to show you, sometimes covering the table in front of you with products in which you have no interest. For Westerners, this kind of shopping experience can be unnerving, because you might feel as though your every move is being scrutinized. Try to avoid being annoyed by this situation; the assistants are merely trying to be helpful. One other thing to consider is that, in the case of many of the craft markets, sales may constitute the shopkeepers' entire source of income, and some traders may come across as overly eager to sell. An expression that may be helpful in such a situation is, *Murakoze, ndimo ndareba gusa* (moo-lah-KOH-zay, NDEE-moh nda-RAY-bah GOO-sah), "Thank you, I'm just looking." If you use this, the vendors are likely to smile and give you space.

You will probably hear prior to your trip that bargaining is a part of Rwandan culture, and that vendors will expect you to haggle. The rule of thumb is this: if the price is marked, there will be less wriggle room. However, that said, if you want to purchase several items you can try offering a slightly lower total figure.

### A Word to the Wise

You should know also that the closer you are to Kigali downtown, where the tourists are, the more the prices will be marked up. At the Kimironko market in Remera (northeast Kigali), I once found three lengths of *kitenge* cloth for 15,000 RwF; the same cloth cost 30,000 RwF at a craft market downtown—a markup of 100 percent! Knowing this, it will not be seen as pushy if you try to negotiate a better price, because you are probably being quoted tourist prices.

It's a good idea to ask a Rwandan (other than the salesperson) what a fair price is, and use this as a baseline. However, if you begin to discuss the price of an item with a vendor (beyond simply asking the price and moving on if you are not interested), and then do *not* purchase the item, the vendor may become visibly upset. This is because in Rwanda entering into a negotiation for price in shopping implies that you will go through with the purchase. Not to do so is insulting and rude.

Finally, it is common in Rwanda to hire porters for market shopping or gorilla trekking. At the larger markets, such as Kimironko, you can expect to be approached by men in yellow vests offering their services. For a Westerner, it may at first seem strange to pay someone to carry your belongings; however, remember that this is an important source of income for the porter, and that Rwandans also hire porters. It is, therefore, both culturally appropriate and economically beneficial to hire one. If you do so, agree on the price beforehand and always make sure to include a tip.

### TIPPING

In restaurants, a tip is not generally expected, though you should leave one for good service, perhaps by rounding up the bill. Other service areas where a tip should be left are guides (local or in one of the natural parks), drivers, hairdressers, massage therapists, porters, and hotel room service staff. A good rule of thumb for tips is to give 5 to 10 percent of the bill, depending on the quality of service you receive.

## SPORTS

Rwandans love sports, as both spectators and participants. Soccer is by far the most popular sport, and you will frequently see children playing improvised games with balls made from plastic bags or, in the provinces, banana leaves. Both in the cities and in the provinces, you can

watch games at soccer pitches or at the larger
stadiums. These are boisterous and enjoyable
affairs, with the crowds avidly cheering their
favorite teams, donning face paint, and blaring
plastic horns.

Other popular sports are cricket, tennis,
basketball, and jogging. It used to be that you

would rarely see Rwandans out for a run, but now more and more people go for early-morning jogs over Rwanda's many hills.

Over the past years, Rwanda's national cycling team has made a worldwide impression, with its growth being detailed in Tim Lewis's book *Land of Second Chances: The Impossible Rise of Rwanda's Cycling Team*, as well the 2012 documentary film *Rising from Ashes*.

## THE ARTS
Rwanda plays host to a vibrant and up-and-coming arts scene. While in Kigali, you should make a visit to the Inema Arts Center, which displays amazing works of visual art, much of which is for sale. The paintings and sculptures here rival the quality of the works of artists anywhere.

Inema Arts Center also holds drumming and dancing sessions twice a week that you can watch free. Among Rwanda's various traditional dance styles the most famous—the expressive Intore dance—is a sight to behold. Originating as a military dance performed in the court of the king (*umwami*), the dance recalls warriors returning from battle armed with spears and shields. The term "Intore" means "chosen ones," signifying those chosen to go off to battle for the king. This later came to mean the select

dancers, whose performance recalls the battle
scenes. It features male dancers jumping and
twisting, and tossing their long, white mane wigs
(made of sisal plant fibers), while the women move
gracefully about in their *imishanana* (skirts with
a sash draped over one shoulder), welcoming the
brave warriors back from combat. This dance will
certainly give you goosebumps. The Iby'Iwacu
Cultural Village in Kinigi (near the boundary of
Volcanoes National Park, just north of Musanze)
regularly holds dance performances for visitors.

Rwanda has a rich musical tradition, with new artists appearing every year. More traditional forms of music include drumming, singing, the *ikembe* (a lamellophone), and the *inanga*, an eight-stringed zither formed over a flat, concave piece

of wood. However, this traditional, precolonial Rwandan music has become more difficult to find, as foreign styles of music have become increasingly prevalent. If you would like to enjoy authentic Rwandan music, you will have to look hard to find it—in libraries, festivals, or at certain weddings. While Western music styles (rap, R&B, twelve-tone chromatic scale, and so on) have influenced Rwandan music, musical styles have also trickled in from neighboring countries, especially as so many Rwandans have repatriated over the years from the diaspora, bringing with them Congolese, Ugandan, Tanzanian, and Burundian music, and more. The contemporary Rwandan music scene now runs the gamut from guitar and jazz to hip-hop, often in English, though quite a few artists perform in Kinyarwanda.

The Rwandan film industry is also growing, with more and more films being made each year in Kinyarwanda. The excellent documentary film, *Finding Hillywood*, offers a glimpse into this growing production.

As for traditional arts, Rwanda's most recognizable craft is the woven basket, variations of which you will find at any craft stand. You can also find woven placemats and floor mats.

Rwandans produce a variety of wood and stone carvings, as well as a vibrantly colored type of painting known as *imigongo*, made from cow dung. The Batwa (or Community of Potters—the politically correct term) are also well known for their handcrafted pottery.

### SOME MUST-SEE TOURIST ATTRACTIONS

Volcanoes National Park: Mountain Gorilla and
Golden Monkey trekking

Akagera National Park

Nyungwe Rainforest

Genocide Memorials: Gisozi Memorial and Museum (Kigali),
Ntarama Church (near Nyamata), the Nyamata Church,
Murambi Technical School

Lake Kivu

The National Museum of Rwanda (Huye/Butare)

Kimironko Market (Kigali)

The Golden Monkeys

# chapter seven

# TRAVEL, HEALTH, & SAFETY

Rwanda's infrastructure is developing at lightning speed. New roads, shiny buildings, and eye-catching new homes pop up seemingly overnight. Not only is Kigali developing, but provincial towns are seeing ever more improvements in roads, buildings, and services. The country has a wide variety of hotels and restaurants, and there is little that you cannot get in Kigali.

However, this is still a developing country, which means that some services or products may be slower to come or not quite what you are used to in more developed countries. This is especially true in the provinces. Every country has its smooth and rough parts, and Rwanda is no exception. Despite great strides over the past twenty years, 30.2 percent of the population were still living in poverty in 2017 (according to *African Economic Outlook*). However, this is down from the reported 2012 rate of 44.9 percent (reported in *Vision 2020*), so the country's economy is still on the rise. Also, do not forget that Rwanda's entire infrastructure, industry, and services sectors were annihilated in 1994. As such, the country has essentially had just over twenty years to achieve its current economic and societal place, which rivals that of many of its neighbors.

## ARRIVAL

Arriving in Rwanda is straightforward and well organized. You fly in to either the Grégoire Kayibanda Airport in Kigali or, starting with its projected opening in 2019, the Bugesera International Airport. For land crossings, you enter through one of the border stations from the DRC, Burundi, Tanzania, or Uganda.

In each case, you will be required to purchase a visa, which cost US $30 in 2017. Persons exempt from visas are nationals from Benin, the Central African Republic, Chad, the DRC, Ghana, Guinea, Indonesia, Haiti, Mauritius, Philippines, Senegal, Seychelles, Sao Tome, Principe, and Singapore.

Citizens from other East African Community countries receive a six-month visitor pass. You may pay for your visa in US dollars (cash) or, if arriving in Kigali, with a credit card. After processing your payment, the border official will give you a payment receipt and stamp your passport with a single-entry visa. Your passport will need to have at least six months' validity remaining for you to be allowed entry.

If you are not being met at the airport by a tour guide, hotel representative, or some other prearranged party, you will find taxis parked in the lot just outside the main entrance. You will also see taxis at the land border crossings. A taxi ride from the airport to downtown Kigali will cost between 3,000 and 5,000 RwF (about US $3.50 to $6.00). A *moto* taxi ride downtown typically runs to about 1,500 RwF. Always agree on a price before entering the taxi. It is wise to avoid unmarked cars posing as taxis.

## GETTING AROUND
### By Car

You must have a valid driver's license to drive in Rwanda. Steering wheels are on the left, and cars drive on the right side of the road. Be aware that speed limits are low compared to those in other parts of the world, and the police are very strict in monitoring these. In the city, the limit is 40 kmph (24.8 mph), while in the countryside it is 60 kmph (37.2 mph).

In Kigali and other cities, streets are well lit at night. In less developed areas, however, the streets can be pitch black. This can prove dangerous for two reasons. First, Rwandan drivers do not always turn on their headlights when night falls (at 6:00 p.m. every day of the year, with darkness fully settled in by about 6:30), or may rely solely on their parking lights. This makes spotting oncoming vehicles more difficult. Second, Rwanda's streets—both in the city and in the country—constantly teem with pedestrians, some of whom walk perilously close to the traffic and are difficult to spot in the dark. Always keep a sharp eye out for pedestrians and oncoming traffic, both day and night. One rule of nighttime driving etiquette: when starting your car or pulling out of a parking lot, turn your headlights on only after you have passed any pedestrians. This prevents the blinding headlights from shining into their eyes.

On two-lane roads, dashed white lines between the two lanes indicate that you may pass; a solid line means that you may not. However, Rwandan drivers tend to overtake aggressively, sometimes on curves or when the line is solid, or when another car or motorcycle is coming from the opposite direction. In the city, be on the lookout for large speed bumps, which are not infrequent. These are sometimes marked with blinking red-and-blue lights implanted directly into the concrete on either side, but not all are visibly marked.

Should you choose to drive in Rwanda, do be aware of these differences, as the driving situation may make for unfamiliar territory and, if you are not used to Rwandan driving, a dangerous one. Especially during rush hour, shortly after night falls, the roads in Kigali can become quite congested, with moto taxis aggressively whipping in between cars, drivers looking for opportunities to pass, and the sidewalks and roadsides full of pedestrians. Because of the unlit roads, the heavy pedestrian traffic, and drivers' tendency to use headlights sparingly, it is best not to drive outside Kigali at night.

In the larger cities and on the country's main roads, you can expect smooth, paved roads. As you wander into smaller urban neighborhoods or stray from the arterials, however, you will encounter dirt roads. During the dry seasons, these become extremely dusty, filling the air with a pink haze and covering everything with a film of red dust, especially in the center and east of the country. When encountering passing cars on dirt roads, you will want to close the windows. Beware of the thick mud and deep ruts that appear during the rainy seasons. If you are heading onto dirt roads during or shortly after the rainy season, a low-riding car is not recommended. Even then, drive slowly and carefully.

### In-Town and Intercity Transportation

In the cities, you will see people walking, taking motos, buses, taxis, and private vehicles. If you are not going far you may choose to walk, but in a city like Kigali be careful: what appears close on a map may take an hour or more to reach on foot. The city is hilly, and your path will wind over and around hills. If you ask directions, a Rwandan may reply that your destination is "just right there," though you may have to walk another hour to get there!

Buses are common, both for in-town and intercity transportation. These look more like large white minivans that stop at marked bus stops or at central bus depots. In a larger city, a bus stop may be recessed from the road and include benches; in the country, you may see only a blue sign with the white letter "P" and a white silhouette of a bus underneath. Many cities in the provinces also have central bus depots that Rwandans refer to as the *gare* ("train station" in French). In Kigali the largest bus station is at Nyabugogo; here you will find buses traveling throughout Kigali and elsewhere in Rwanda. This is not the only bus depot, however;

one in Nyanza (just south of Kicukiro) serves routes heading south; the Remera Bus Park serves many buses heading east; while the Kimironko Bus Park serves general intercity buses within Kigali. To avoid going to the wrong one, it's advisable first to ask where in town you need to go to take the bus to your destination.

When you arrive at the *gare*, ask around for your bus by saying, *Ibisi* [name of your destination] *ari hehe?* (ee-BEE-syee AH-lee HAY-HAY). To ask for a bus to Nyamirambo then, you would say, *Ibisi Nyamirambo ari hehe?* Generally people will be helpful in directing you to the correct spot, possibly even leading you there by hand. If you are traveling by bus within the city itself, someone will typically announce the bus's destination from the side door when it pulls up to the bus stop. At the *gares*, you will also see a number of counters and stalls for individual bus companies such as RFTC, City Express, Volcano Express, Capital Express, and so on. You may purchase your ticket here. You then board your bus and give your receipt to the ticket collector, who is also the driver's assistant. You can also simply board your bus and pay in cash before the bus leaves.

To request a stop, tap on the window with your knuckle or a coin. You can also tell the driver where you are going beforehand, and he will remember your stop and let you know when you arrive. If you have a large bag, the assistant will help you load it into the rear of the van, where he will slide it under the back seat.

The moto taxis are one of the most noticeable types of in-town transportation. In any city, it is impossible not to see one wherever you look, day or night. If you are out walking, you need never worry about getting lost— you can always take a moto taxi to your destination.

Simply put, moto taxis are motorcycles designed to carry a single passenger—though you may sometimes see two passengers on a single moto. You can recognize them by the drivers' red or yellow vests and green helmets adorned with a phone number. The drivers each carry a spare helmet, which they offer you when you mount. Moto taxis are extremely convenient and cheap, with a ride from the Kigali suburbs to the center costing about 1,500 RwF.

### Moto Madness

There is, however, something to be said
about safety. Moto accidents are frequent,
and the maintenance of the individual motos
is questionable. I have taken many motos in
Rwanda, and only two of these had a functional
speedometer; on several I have had to rest my
right foot on the muffler. Moreover, moto drivers
here are not known for being sedate. They zip in
and out of traffic, weaving perilously close to cars
as they zoom through traffic circles. While riding
motos is convenient, be aware of the risks. Your
insurance policy may not cover accidents
incurred when riding a moto.

You will also find taxis in Rwanda's cities. These
are generally parked at the airport, bus depots,
and border crossings. Taxis are marked, and it
is advisable to avoid unmarked cars touting for
business. Of the different forms of transport, taxis
tend to be more expensive. Before boarding, tell
your driver where you want to go and agree on
the price. It is not uncommon for a foreigner to
be quoted a higher price than would be offered
a Rwandan. A good idea would be first to ask a
Rwandan (for example, at your hotel) what a fair
price to your destination would be and then to
negotiate accordingly. If you walk away from a
cab driver offering you a price that, according

to another Rwandan, is too high, there is a good chance that he will agree to your price in the end.

For longer journeys in the provinces, you can also hire a private driver. You can do this either through a reputable tour operator or your hotel may be able to reserve a driver for you. In the latter case, it is a good idea to have a Rwandan call and agree on the price for you before engaging the driver. In the case of a private driver, you should add a tip to the agreed-upon fee.

## WHERE TO STAY

Accommodation varies from the frugal to the highly lavish. Four-star hotels in the larger cities rival the quality of any hotels elsewhere, with such amenities as swimming pools, world-class dining, bars, and spa services. You will also find more budget-oriented hotels and guest houses with basic services including, sometimes, your daily water being provided in a small bucket. Between these extremes there is a wide range of options.

On the simpler side, you can sometimes rent rooms in a convent or monastery. These can be quite affordable, and a good option when farther afield. Some individuals rent out private rooms at a reasonable price, and several online organizations can connect you with home-stays. Choosing one of these may be your best bet if you wish to come into more contact with locals, but remember that the person may simply be renting their space for the extra income, and not necessarily to meet and interact with visitors. Still, such accommodation offers a more personal touch. If you are a first-time visitor to Rwanda it is unlikely that you will be invited to stay in someone's home. This may only occur after a friendship has had time to develop.

On the higher end of the scale, you will find a choice of luxury lodges designed to attract an eco-tourist-minded, elite clientele. These are mostly found near or in the larger national parks (Volcanoes National Park, Nyungwe Forest, and Akagera National Park). While cheaper options such as tent camps do exist, Rwanda has recently opened such opulent offerings as Bisate Lodge in Volcanoes National Park, with rooms available from $1,155 to $1,470 USD (£862 to £1,097) per night. Whether you choose a more budget-oriented or high-end lodge, these can be an excellent base for wildlife trekking, birding, or going on safari. Whatever your budget, Rwanda can offer accommodation to suit your needs.

## HEALTH

Rwanda has a universal health care system. Depending on their income, Rwandans pay on a gradated scale into the national Mutuelle de Santé, a national health coverage program. This serves as a sort of insurance, offsetting medical costs. All health care must be paid for upfront and in cash. Except in rare instances, Rwandans will typically opt to see a trained health care professional, rather than rely on traditional healing techniques.

When Rwandans fall ill or need to see a doctor, they will head either to a clinic (*Centre de Santé*) or to a hospital, such as the King Faisal or Kanombe Military Hospital in Kigali. *Centres de Santé* can be found throughout Rwanda. For more immediate assistance they will call an ambulance. For emergencies, one can call 112 on the phone. This is a general emergency number, and the operator can connect the caller with an ambulance; otherwise, a patient would call the hospital directly, as the hospitals dispatch their own ambulances.

The hospitals in Rwanda treat a wide variety of ailments. However, space can sometimes be lacking, which may lead to patients having to wait for an available bed or be sent elsewhere for treatment. For more serious or protracted conditions, patients may seek specialized care elsewhere, such as Kenya, South Africa, or even India.

Before leaving for Rwanda, check with your doctor about country-specific vaccine recommendations as these can change over time. Furthermore, be sure to check current safety recommendations with your country's foreign affairs department, as these too can change. The recommendations here are by no means exhaustive; they are meant only to provide some general considerations regarding health and safety.

As we've seen, if you go to a doctor or hospital in Rwanda you must pay out-of-pocket. International travelers need to check with their home insurance providers about coverage abroad. If you receive treatment in the country, the Rwandan doctor should provide you with paperwork to submit to your insurance provider when you return home.

The Rwandan Ministry of Health used to require proof of yellow fever vaccination for all international travelers entering the country. Now, this vaccine is required only of travelers coming from yellow-fever-endemic locales, including the bordering countries of the DRC, Burundi, Tanzania, and Uganda. You may also be required to show proof of vaccination if entering these countries. The Centers for Disease Control (CDC) does, however, recommend yellow fever vaccination for those planning on spending a longer amount of time in the country. The CDC also recommends that, beyond getting routine vaccinations such as MMR, diphtheria-tetanus, varicella, polio, and flu, most travelers be vaccinated for Hepatitis A and typhoid, and that visitors take a prescription anti-malarial prophylaxis. If your travels will bring you into close contact with animals, then the CDC recommends a rabies vaccine as well.

## Health Hazards
### Gastrointestinal
Your most likely health issue in Rwanda will be gastrointestinal—in the form of travelers' diarrhea or food poisoning. The former is typically

transmitted through poor hygiene from food handlers or from food that has not been properly (that is, hygienically) prepared.

To protect yourself, wash your hands religiously and make frequent use of hand sanitizer. Avoid eating unpeeled fruit or vegetables. All food should be thoroughly cooked and hot when you eat it. Do not eat rare or medium-rare meats, and avoid game meats altogether. You will see many buffets in Rwanda; it's a good idea to steer clear of salads or other food that is at room temperature or not hot, or food that has been washed in water. It is not recommended to eat food from street vendors.

Even though the water in Kigali is treated, drink only bottled water, as your stomach will probably not be used to the difference in water. Use bottled water as well for brushing your teeth and whenever you need to put water in your mouth. If you order a cocktail in a restaurant or bar, make sure that the ice cubes are made from bottled or purified water.

Finally, it is common practice in Rwanda for bottled drinks (beer, Fanta, tonic, and so on) to be opened in front of you. If someone brings you a bottled drink that has already been opened, you should send it back and request another.

### Malaria

Malaria is transmitted by infected mosquitoes—insects that become active from dusk to dawn. There is no vaccine against malaria, but you should see your doctor to obtain the appropriate anti-malarial prophylaxis to take while in the country. Make sure to research the different types of medication to find the one that suits your constitution best, as some of the medications can have negative side effects. It is very important that you take your medication while in Rwanda, as malaria can be deadly.

You should also take measures to avoid contact with mosquitoes: wear a DEET-based insect repellent, cover exposed skin with long sleeves and pants, and always sleep under a mosquito net. In some places in Rwanda—for example, in air-conditioned hotels in Kigali or in the higher elevations in the north—your bed may not have a mosquito net. This is because air conditioning typically controls mosquitoes in a room, and mosquitoes avoid higher, colder altitudes. According to the CDC, the incubation period for malaria is from seven to thirty days, though this could be longer for someone who has taken anti-malarial prophylaxis; this can cause misdiagnoses. Therefore, if you have any flu-like symptoms or nausea even weeks after you leave, be sure to tell your doctor that you have been in Rwanda.

*Schistosomiasis/Bilharzia*
While in Rwanda, avoid swimming, wading, or washing in fresh water such as rivers, lakes, streams, and marshes. Not only are there crocodiles in the Nyabarongo River and other lakes and rivers (in fact, seven people in Kigali

were killed by crocodiles in the Nyabarongo during the summer of 2017), but fresh water can be host to the bilharzia parasite. Living in water contaminated by human and animal waste, the bilharzia parasite can enter human bodies through the skin. While bilharzia is treatable, it can make you quite ill.

*Tsetse Flies*
According to the World Health Organization, there is no risk of sleeping sickness (trypanosomiasis) in Rwanda—a disease transmitted by infected tsetse flies. This does not, however, prevent the insects from being a nuisance, interrupting a pleasant safari with their painful bites. If you are planning a trip to Akagera National Park, you can take measures to avoid the tsetse's bite by wearing a DEET-based insect repellent and not wearing blue, black, or dark colors, which attract the flies.

*HIV*
The incidence of HIV in Rwanda is dropping and, according to UNAIDS, had stabilized in 2015 at 0.11 percent. Despite these positive gains, the traveler should never take unnecessary sexual risks while abroad. Always take measures to reduce your exposure to HIV, including using a condom and avoiding too much alcohol, as alcohol impairs judgment. It should also go without saying that you should avoid sharing needles, razors, or any other devices that have come into contact with another person's bodily fluids.

## SAFETY AND SECURITY

As we saw in the Introduction, Rwanda is one of the safest countries in the world for tourists and businesses, ranking ninth in place according to the World Economic Forum (a rank that does not consider petty crime). For comparison, the United States ranks 84th, and the United Kingdom 78th.

In Rwanda the visitor immediately gets the sense of a safe and secure environment—both urban and rural. Police and armed military guards maintain a visible watch on streets, the cities and countryside remain impeccably clean, and traffic speed limits are almost draconically low in an effort to curb road accidents. According to the US State Department, violent crime against foreigners is extremely rare, and those cases you read about are—in the context of their incidence in relation to the population—statistically almost insignificant.

The main threat of violence that could affect foreigners seems, according to reports by international government agencies, to stem not from Rwanda itself, but from the neighboring DRC. Indeed, the Kivu and North Kivu Provinces of the DRC (the two closest to the northwest Rwandan border, near Gisenyi) have, over the past two decades, seen their fair share of violent activity involving various rebel groups, some of whom consist of former *génocidaires* who fled Rwanda in 1994. Most recently in February 2018, fighting erupted between Rwandan and Congolese forces just inside the DRC, and violence has in the past spilled over Rwanda's border. While Gisenyi and the Volcanoes National Park are both beautiful examples of urban and natural vistas, the visitor would be wise to monitor conditions on the DRC side of Lake Kivu, as trouble can flare up quickly.

Throughout Rwanda, though, the main threats to safety and security come from pickpocketing and petty theft. While traffic safety has been a major issue in the past, new laws, as well as strict (and low) speed limits, have seriously improved motorists' and pedestrians' safety. Regarding theft, the visitor should exercise a modicum of common sense: never leaving valuables in sight (say, in a parked car); keeping your wallet or purse close to you, especially in crowded areas; not attracting undue attention to yourself; avoiding poorly lit areas at night; and in general avoiding secluded places and areas with which you are unfamiliar.

---

**USEFUL TELEPHONE NUMBERS**
**Police or ambulance  112**
**To report a traffic accident  113**
**To report police misconduct  116**

# BUSINESS
# BRIEFING

# chapter eight

## THE BUSINESS CLIMATE

Over the past twenty years Rwanda has become a
country that welcomes business and investment.
With its rapid development, the opportunities
for business abound. To encourage business,
the Rwandan government has streamlined the
bureaucratic side of entrepreneurship. The
online portals at the Rwandan Development

Board (www.rdb.rw) offer a straightforward and user-friendly interface to process paperwork to register new businesses. Indeed, applying for a business permit takes just a day to complete. Prior to setting up your business in Rwanda, however, you will also have to register with the Rwanda Revenue Authority (www.rra.gov.rw), which governs taxation. Doing so will allow you to plan adequately for paying the appropriate labor taxes. Moreover, you should also check with your home country's tax authority, as income earned in Rwanda could be taxed at home. Finally, you will need to file employer registration with the Rwanda Social Security Board (www.rssb.rw).

When you are entering Rwanda from the DRC, one of the first signs you see is a large billboard bearing the message, "Investment yes, corruption no." Another huge boost to the healthy business atmosphere is Rwanda's zero tolerance of corruption. According to Transparency International, Rwanda ranks 50/176 in terms of Corruption Perception, with a score of 54 percent, at the same time ranking as sub-Saharan Africa's third-least-corrupt

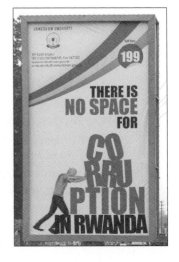

country. One Rwandan once quipped that corruption was punished as strictly as murder. While this may be a great exaggeration, it illustrates how seriously Rwandans take preventing and eliminating corruption at all levels of society.

One area in which Rwanda is still making strides is what one might call "professionalism." In 1994 almost an entire generation of potential entrepreneurs and professionals was eliminated in one of the most brutal and efficient genocides in history. Rwanda's recovery has been truly amazing, but this tragedy has meant that professionals have had a delayed start compared to other world economies. One Rwandan explained that the country is like a car that has had a massive breakdown whose driver is pressing the gas to the floor to catch up with the others in the race. The understanding of service and professionalism is, therefore, still growing compared to other countries' professional sectors. It can happen, for example, that someone may be promoted to a leadership position who does not yet have the fully developed skills to execute the job. This may also contribute to behavior that Westerners might find frustrating, such as delayed or no replies to correspondence, texting, or taking personal calls at work or during meetings, or not initiating tasks that were not explicitly asked for by a supervisor. Always remember Rwanda's larger historical context when doing business here, and never forget to be patient, respectful, and deferential to your Rwandan counterparts.

## DEALING WITH THE GOVERNMENT

Depending on your business in Rwanda, it is likely that you will interact with government ministries or representatives at some point. Here are a few tips to smooth your path.

First, although Rwanda offers a very business-friendly climate, it is a highly regulated country, and at every level of government Rwandans take regulations seriously. The rules are the rules; never expect someone in the government to make an exception for you or to pull strings to speed up the process. Even though you may feel frustrated by some of the regulations, giving vent to your frustration—especially to government officials—would be likely to backfire and cause your Rwandan counterparts to shut down to you. Remain friendly and patient at all times.

In dealing with the government you must respect the strict hierarchy of decision-making, and before any of your projects are approved they will need to go through each step of the hierarchy. For projects of greater import to the country, approval will need to come from even higher up—perhaps at the cabinet level. Do not expect one individual to be able to sign off on your project. Getting this approval takes time and patience. Furthermore, your project may be delayed if matters of greater importance cross the desk of the official whose support you need. It is not for you to dictate what gets done when.

Any person wishing to do business in Rwanda would do well to read two government documents that essentially constitute Rwanda's mission and vision. These are *Vision 2020* and the *EDPRS II*. At every level of the government, these documents guide decision- and policy-making. Furthermore, there is a great deal of accountability placed on local and national officials—in the form of performance contracts (*imihigo*) between officials and the president—to meet the targets laid out. You can access these *imihigo* on the City of Rwanda Web site (www.kigalicity.gov.rw), under "Publications." What this means is that, in dealing with government representatives, your chances for success will increase if you frame your requests or proposals in terms of *Vision 2020* and the *EDPRS*. Do your business goals align with those laid out in these two documents? Will your business support an official's own goals as laid out in his or her performance contract? In other words, are your goals in line with the country's goals? Do you perceive a gap in a sector's achieving these goals that you could help to fill? And, if so, can you offer a solution that is responsive to Rwanda's needs? Will you be a positive force in helping Rwanda achieve *Vision 2020* and the *EDPRS*?

This does not mean that you will have no chance of success if your goals are not within those laid out in *Vision 2020* and the *EDPRS*. What it means is that if your goals align with those of the government representatives who must sign off on your project, then a government official may more quickly see how your goal and theirs (and, by extension, Rwanda's) align. In other words, your venture should focus on what Rwanda and Rwandans need, not solely on what you need.

## BUSINESS CULTURE

Beyond the issue of professionalism, an interesting cultural phenomenon is, to use the words of one businessperson in Rwanda, the "culture of the stamp." Any official document in Rwanda—indeed, any document of importance—will be rubber-stamped and signed by the relevant official or businessperson. (Once, when visiting a rural school, the author noticed that the director had affixed the school's stamp over his signature on a simple handwritten note regarding schedules.) The stamp is a sign of value and importance. While your home company or government may not apply rubber stamps so faithfully, your documents will probably be taken more seriously if they do have an official rubber stamp. If your company does possess such a stamp, affixing it at the signature line of any official correspondence will increase your chances of your letter being taken seriously.

An element of any business or government entity that the visitor will notice is that Rwandans place a great deal of importance on rank and position. When you communicate with someone, you should be aware of their place in the hierarchy, which you should respect. Do they possess a title? If so, you should use it when you address the person, and in all correspondence. If a decision flows up the hierarchy, you should not attempt to bypass anyone in order to get a decision more quickly. To do so runs the risk of those at the lower levels seeing your move as rude; they may become reluctant to deal with you in the future, or they may even obstruct your requests. This could have significant consequences, as their position as gatekeepers to the organization's hierarchy could hinder future dealings. Also, if one person in the chain does not approve of some element of your query or project, it is unlikely that your approval will proceed up the hierarchy.

Finally, to increase your chances of success when doing business in Rwanda you must demonstrate that you are committed to Rwanda in the long term. If your objectives align with the government's you will be more likely to find support for your enterprise. There are great possibilities for business and innovation in Rwanda, but you should avoid appearing to be purely self-serving. It must be clear throughout all of your business dealings that you are sincerely interested in contributing to Rwanda's stated goals, as dictated by performance contracts, *Vision 2020*, and the *EDPRS II*.

## DRESS CODE

If you are doing business in Rwanda, you most definitely need to be seen as "serious." Opinions about you tend to form instantly, and they can flavor your entire relationship. Positive first impressions can be helpful in doing business, while negative first impressions can be difficult to overcome. If Rwandans perceive you as not being "serious," they may clam up or be unresponsive to your queries. Rwandans even have an expression for this. In French, one is or is not *sérieux*, whereas in Kinyarwanda the expression for a person who is "serious" is *Umuntu ukomeje kucyemezo yafashe*, meaning, "A person who keeps his word."

One of the first ways in which someone is regarded as "serious" or "not serious" is in their dress. If you show up wearing creased pants, a tee shirt, or sneakers, you will not be seen as

"serious." You should strive to dress nicely for meetings, your hair should be neat, and men should be clean-shaven. For men, appropriate clothing would be pressed slacks, polished dress shoes, and a pressed, collared shirt—ties can be optional, depending on the occasion, as are smart jackets. For women, a pressed business dress that descends below the knee and that does not reveal shoulders is appropriate. Rwandans place a great deal of importance on personal appearance, and if you do not seem to take care of your personal appearance, how can you be "serious"? And, by extension, why should I give you any of my time?

## SETTING UP A BUSINESS MEETING

If you are trying to set up a meeting from outside Rwanda, a good way to begin would be to have a Rwandan intermediary inside the country initiate contact through a direct phone call, which would both help to build trust and allow initial connections. This may not always be possible, however. If you attempt to set up a meeting yourself, remember that patience and friendly persistence are your keys to success.

You may start with an e-mail or a phone call. Begin speaking in English, which has become the lingua franca of business. If appropriate, you may switch to French. Introduce yourself and explain how your requested meeting can be of benefit to the Rwandan counterpart. It is not unlikely that you will get no answer to your e-mail—or you will receive initial replies to your e-mails, but then, unexpectedly, your contact ceases to respond. If this happens, follow up by phone or in person.

When phoning, introduce yourself politely and explain why you would like a meeting. You may also ask when a good time would be to stop by in person. It is unlikely that you would achieve a meeting on the first try. The person may need to check into schedules or with their superior. If they tell you to call back, make sure to do so; and if they say that they will check for you, be sure to continue phoning back after a day or two, always remaining friendly as you remind the person of who you are and why you are requesting a meeting. Communicating via texting and Whatsapp is common, and these forms of communication are generally not seen as unprofessional when used during the day.

If you are in Rwanda, it is fine to show up to an office in person to introduce yourself and request a meeting. Dress well, and have a business card to present. When you meet the secretary or other first point of contact, ask when a good time to come back would be, and then be persistent and friendly in your continued efforts to set up a meeting. Be prepared to make several return trips to set up a meeting, or to wait onsite until the person whom you wish to meet becomes available. No matter the outcome of your first encounter with a secretary or other professional, be persistent and friendly in your follow-ups. If someone says that they will get back to you, it is not inappropriate to follow up a few days later.

If you are trying to set up a meeting with a government official, you should begin with a formal letter, explaining your reasons for the meeting. Ideally, your letter should also include language from the official's own performance contract (*imihigo*). This would further demonstrate how your goals align with the official's (and Rwanda's) goals. After the letter, follow up with e-mails and phone calls.

## MEETINGS

Prior to your meeting, make sure to follow up frequently by phone or texting to confirm the time and place. You may even confirm on the day of the meeting, and even on your way there. It is not unheard of for people not to show up at a meeting that has been agreed on. Be prepared for meetings to be canceled at the last minute, with or without warning. This can occur because something more important has come up that is outside the person's control, such as rain, or their being required to do something else by a superior. If the meeting is canceled, remain friendly and patient, and begin the process of setting up another time and place.

At a meeting, you should greet everyone with a handshake, eye contact, and *Muraho. Amakuru?* ("Hello, how are you?"), unless there are very many people. Present a business card to everyone there, unless the meeting is large, in which case be sure to hand cards to the relevant decision-makers and organizers.

Be prepared for meetings to last much longer than you expect. During the meeting itself, it is not uncommon to see people texting or even taking calls on their cell phones. It can happen that someone not only takes a call, but has the conversation in the same room as the meeting.

## PRESENTATIONS

If you are giving a presentation, speak slowly and insert pauses. Clear visuals are helpful, especially ones that list the salient points, so that attendees can have a visual summary of the contents. In addition to any posters or slides you may show, provide a handout with all of your main points— even a transcript of your presentation will be helpful, especially since English is unlikely to be the first language of your audience. In Rwanda, extemporaneous or creative public speaking is less common than in the West, and meetings often feature a presenter who reads their PowerPoint presentation word for word.

When giving a presentation, ask what the time frame is. Do you have thirty minutes? An hour? Two hours? Before you begin, you should publicly acknowledge the presence of any VIPs in attendance, thanking them respectfully and using their titles. Speak slowly and insert ample pauses. If the meeting was called at your instigation, also publicly thank all of those in the hierarchy who made it possible. Thank them for their generous time and effort in setting up the meeting, and emphasize how you look forward to collaboration.

You can also set parameters for how you will field questions. May audience members interrupt? Or would you prefer to answer questions at the end? Don't be surprised if you are interrupted, however. Be prepared as well to engage in small talk about family, and so on, before getting to the point. Sometimes meetings can seem to filled with apparently insignificant topics—family, weather, sports, travel—before getting down to the business at hand only within the last ten or fifteen minutes.

Whatever the nature of your pitch, it always a good idea to acknowledge that you understand the successes that the Rwandan organization or business has enjoyed, and explain how you would like to help their organization meet its goals. If its goals and yours fall in line with *Vision 2020*, the *EDPRS II*, or a local official's performance contract (*imihigo*), make sure to stress this. Another element that is important in doing business is validation. If your ideas or project have already received validation from someone in the government or someone higher in the organization, mention this; this stresses that the key players see value in what you are offering. If you are seeking approval for a project, it will have to be validated—usually in writing—by every level up the hierarchy before getting to the top.

## NEGOTIATIONS

Everything in Rwanda is a negotiation—not in the business sense, but rather in the sense of two or more people communicating at length to reach common ground. In Rwanda, negotiations are highly consensual; your goal should be that both parties clearly benefit. One thing to remember when engaging in any sort of negotiation—

from a taxi fare to a business venture—is to keep it personal and human. You are dealing with a human being with needs and wants, and not with a nameless face or bureaucrat. As such, search for personal commonalities: do you and the other person have a shared acquaintance? Have you traveled to the same place or experienced the same event? Is there something you can laugh about together? Or is there something unique about Rwandan culture that you would like to know more about? Asking about Rwandan culture in a curious or interested way may lead the person to open up and beam with pride at your interest, thus establishing a more personal connection and trust.

As with the meetings, you can expect negotiations in Rwanda to be lengthier and more involved than you may be used to. Furthermore, when negotiating, Rwandans tend to focus on finding a mutually beneficial outcome. Pushiness rarely works, and neither does inflexibility; rather, each party will seek to achieve its own goals while also keeping the others' goals in mind. In America, for example, negotiations tend to be aggressive and, at times, confrontational. "Take it or leave it," can be the mantra. In Rwanda, such an approach might be successful in the short term, but not in the long term. Being pushy or too demanding runs the risk of having people shut down and become intractable. You also may be seen as rude, or, even worse, as trying to take advantage of Rwandans as a privileged outsider.

Your chances of success in negotiations will increase if you first remember that negotiations are about finding mutually beneficial outcomes. Second, focus on long-term business relationships as opposed to short-term gains. Third, clearly articulate how your objectives align with Rwanda's objectives. If you are involved in protracted negotiations, make sure to punctuate your business communications with messages of good wishes or simple greetings to the other people and their families. It is vital, however, that such communications be sincere; don't take a cynical approach and offer the guise of developing a relationship for the sake of business. It will soon be sensed!

Finally, no matter what frustrations you may feel, never argue or lose your patience. This may cause people to shut down or skirt the issue. Arguing and losing your patience can cause your Rwandan counterparts to feel as though they are losing face; it can also cause them to see you as being pushy and rude. Rather than lose your patience, acknowledge that you are appreciative of your counterparts' time and energy, and apologize for any inconvenience that you may have caused. This shows deference to Rwandan culture and also that you are agreeing to play by Rwandans' rules.

## CONTRACTS AND FULFILLMENT

The Rwandan legal code is partly inherited from the Belgians, partly common law. In recent years the Rwandan government has taken further steps to develop contract laws that are more directly modeled on common law. The crux of contract laws is to define what constitutes a contract, as well as to stipulate the conditions according to which contracts may or may not be enforced, and the conditions defining legal labor. In other words, they explain in general terms what constitutes a contract or a breach of contract, as well as who would be indebted to whom in case of a breach. However, they do not enumerate the specifics of how one determines if a breach has occurred, especially in the case of breaches stemming from differing interpretations.

Because of this, it is wise to draft contracts that are as specific as possible in their vocabulary, terms, and conditions, so that all parties are fully covered; they should clearly and specifically define what is expected of all signatories. To avoid misunderstandings, contracts should be written in Kinyarwanda and English or French, and they should be signed and stamped by all parties involved. Moreover, it is important that written agreements show that both parties are benefiting; the agreement should not be one-sided. For written contracts, it would be wise to consult a Rwandan lawyer who can help you to navigate the legal intricacies.

Depending on the weight of the contract, trust and personal relationships play varying roles. For lighter or verbal contracts (such as agreements to buy a product or provide a service in the short term), written contracts are not always produced; under Rwandan law, smaller-scale and lower-priced purchase contracts may be verbal. Should a disagreement arise in such a contract, the disagreement is usually mitigated through trust and discussion, as opposed to arbitration or other legal resolution. Moreover, smaller-scale contracts are rarely considered sacrosanct; rather, there is a good deal of flexibility on both sides, as long as the parties agree. Deadlines and terms can be flexible, and it is rare to find two parties adhering rigidly to the letter of the agreement.

As contracts become weightier, however, the written document acquires more weight, especially in cases in which the parties are not friends or acquaintances. Rwandan law requires written contracts for any employment exceeding ninety days and for any sale exceeding 50,000 RwF.

In general, Rwandans, being a highly non-confrontational people, prefer to settle contract or labor disagreements interpersonally and amicably; and then they may choose to sweep a disagreement under the rug if it is deemed less important than preserving face or causing further disagreements by bringing it up. Still, if contract disagreements cannot be resolved, or if they are worth more, Rwandans may take their case to an arbitration center such as the Kigali International Arbitration Centre (www.kiac.org. rw). Because of heavy backlogs in the Rwandan courts, such extra-legal services as these (and, at the district level, the *abunzi*, see below) exist to resolve conflicts efficiently. Should mediation not work, however, contract disputes may proceed to the Primary Court (in the case of civil disputes) or to the Labor Inspectorate (in the case of labor disputes).

## MANAGING DISAGREEMENTS

That Rwandans are highly conflict-averse can be seen in their communication styles (such as the "Rwandan no," and speaking in code or around topics), in their outward reserve, in their suppressing shows of emotion, and in the way they negotiate disagreements.

It is extremely rare for one Rwandan to confront another directly about a perceived fault or problem. Doing so would be substantially to compromise face. Rather, Rwandans might only hint at the problem or, as is more often the case, they would talk about the problem to a third person, who may relay the issue to the second party (and then, likely, indirectly). Such approaches to conflict permeate all levels of Rwandan interactions, from the interpersonal and informal to the professional milieu. In fact, it is not uncommon for Rwandans to suppress disagreements altogether, even in the workplace.

When conflicts persist, however, Rwandans can find help in the *abunzi*. These are cell- and sector-level conflict mediators composed of seven (non-government) persons from the area chosen for their trustworthiness and fairness, and who mediate conflicts not exceeding 3,000,000 RwF in cost or potential damages. According to the Rwandan Ministry of Justice Web site, conflicts must first be addressed by the *abunzi* before they can go to trial. The *abunzi* sessions are held publicly. Each side presents its case without a lawyer, and the seven *abunzi* deliberate before rendering a decision. The majority of cases brought before the *abunzi* tend to be land disputes.

# chapter nine

# COMMUNICATING

## LANGUAGE

Rwanda has four official languages: Kinyarwanda, English, Swahili, and French. Of these, all Rwandans speak Kinyarwanda, a Bantu language related to Swahili. Kinyarwanda is a language consisting of sixteen noun classes (like genders in Romance languages) and three tones. Learning Kinyarwanda outside Rwanda is challenging, owing to the lack of materials, though their number is growing. Despite the challenge, though, investing time in learning some Kinyarwanda before your visit is well worth

the effort. Rwandans always welcome attempts to speak their language. In doing so you also convey your respect and deference to Rwandan culture, and people are likely to warm to you more quickly. That said, you may find that, while you begin a conversation in Kinyarwanda, Rwandans will soon switch to English or French.

Until 2008, all secondary instruction in Rwanda was in French. As a result, French is commonly spoken in many areas of the country, particularly among the older generations. This is all the more true when you leave Kigali, as many people in the provinces speak French. In 2008, though, the language of instruction switched almost overnight to English. In the cities, you will regularly find people who speak English and who can help you. This is especially true in places of business and government offices. One minor note is that the English vocabulary you hear will be British rather than American— Rwandans will speak of "football" instead of "soccer," the "lift" instead of the "elevator," and so on. Rwandans may also confuse Ls and Rs in spoken English, as the two sounds are interchangeable in Kinyarwanda. You may even see "Kigali" spelled "Kigari," and "Ryangombe" as "Lyangombe."

Swahili—the lingua franca in East-Central Africa—is widely understood and spoken throughout Rwanda, with many Swahili expressions peppering Kinyarwanda: *karibu* ("weclome"), *sawa* ("okay"), *Ni saa angape?* ("What time is it?"), as well as other expressions for telling the time. If you speak Swahili, you will find that the Swahili spoken in western Rwanda is closer to Congolese Swahili, which, in addition to variations in pronunciation, is heavily influenced by French and Lingala. In the east, however, the Swahili spoken will more closely resemble that spoken in other East African countries, such as Tanzania and Kenya.

## FORMS OF ADDRESS

If you meet someone who introduces themselves by their first name, it is generally acceptable to continue on a first-name basis. Be careful, though, as Rwandans have two names: a Kinyarwanda name given to them shortly after birth and a (typically English or French) Christian name. In Rwanda, family names do not pass on as they do in Western countries; likewise, a married woman does not take her husband's name. The Kinyarwanda name is chosen by the parents for its meaning; typically, it reflects hopes for the child or perhaps the conditions of the pregnancy or birth. Thus, you may see a name such as Olivier Bizimana, where "Bizimana" means "only God knows." Because each child receives a different name from his or her parents, Bizimana's sister's name could well be Habimana Claudette, "God exists." Rwandans often present or write their names beginning with the Kinyarwanda name; thus: Bizimana Olivier. The key is to listen carefully when introductions are made and follow the Rwandans' lead, using the name that the person presents to you.

If a person is an official or some other title-holder (such as Director, Principal, Officer, and so on) there are two considerations. First, you are likely to be introduced to the person by someone else, and you should allow the person in question to initiate handshakes and introductions. It is polite and respectful to let them first address you before you initiate a conversation. Second, it is important to include any titles when addressing them. Thus, when meeting a government official, you might say, "Honorable Bizimana Olivier," "Mr. Director," or "Teacher." Always err on the side of being too formal rather than less formal. You will hear older or elderly Rwandan men referred to as *mzee* (pronounced "muh-ZAY"), and elderly women referred to as "mama." These are title of high respect—or, in the case of younger men calling each other *mzee*, mockery!

Finally, if you are speaking French to your counterparts, always use the formal *vous*, unless the Rwandans invite you to use *tu*.

## BODY LANGUAGE

As we have seen, body language plays an important role. As a general rule, the Rwandan notion of personal space tends to be smaller than that of some Western cultures. Rwandans may stand closer to you than you are used to, and they may speak softly, especially in public. If, out of a wider sense of personal space, a foreigner steps away from a Rwandan who stands close to talk, this could give rise to a cultural misunderstanding. By backing away you may cause your Rwandan counterpart to assume that there is some reason for this. Did he do something to offend you? Do you want to avoid him?

Remember that Rwandans are more likely to maintain physical contact—typically by holding your hand or arm—while talking or showing you something. Handshakes last much longer, and a Rwandan is likely to keep hold while you speak.

It is more common to see Rwandans of the same sex holding hands or arms in public than it is to see heterosexual duos holding hands; there is nothing sexual or romantic about such contact. It is merely a way of expressing friendship and trust.

Rwandans also will typically not maintain eye contact during a discussion, as to do so could be seen as overly forward or aggressive. They typically glance at their interlocutor at the beginning of the conversation, and then look away or slightly to the side. This is not ignoring you or maintaining an impersonal distance; it is a means of conflict avoidance.

## JOKES AND HUMOR

Rwandans enjoy a good laugh with friends or acquaintances. The Rwandan sense of humor is largely based on shared experiences, or it is situational: Rwandans might laugh at some shared experience, referred to directly or indirectly. It is not uncommon for Rwandans to tease each other, even making inside jokes that only certain friends "get." If one person does something embarrassing, for example, friends may bring this up in later conversations for a laugh.

Rwandan humor is often linguistic, especially among adults and older people. Proverbs, puns, and riddles play an important role in Rwandan culture. To make a humorous point, then, a Rwandan might use a riddle to suggest something funny or, rather than answer a question directly, will answer a question with a riddle (the answer to which is the answer to the question posed). For an outsider, cracking into this sort of humor will prove highly difficult, as it requires not only fluent Kinyarwanda, but also an intimate familiarity with how proverbs and riddles are used.

### Where is It?

For the visitor, self-deprecating humor can be helpful in breaking the ice. This is especially true when mentioning your faux pas in trying to learn and appreciate Rwandan culture. As an example, I was once eating lunch at one of the finest hotels in Kigali. Though the staff all spoke English, I insisted on asking for the restrooms in Kinyarwanda: *Umusarani ari he?* The waiter, however, gaped at my question. I tried again, and received another blank expression. I then asked for the restroom in English, and the waiter immediately showed me the way. Later, I learned that I had actually asked for the "pit latrine"—something unlikely to be found at a luxury hotel! I have mentioned this to several Rwandans since, and they have all found it knee-slappingly funny.

There are some types of humor that you will not find in Rwanda. Rwandans do not typically tell jokes of the setup–punchline variety, and sarcasm is also likely to backfire. In a similar vein, slapstick and scatological humor are seen as silly and, in the case of the latter, vulgar. Political humor and satire are also absent; you should avoid making satirical or humorous comments about any political leaders, be they Rwandan or from elsewhere. Mocking or disparaging political leaders is taboo in Rwanda.

## TECHNOLOGY

Rwandans are tech-savvy (especially the younger generations), and most possess one or more cell phones. Texting is ubiquitous, and is not inappropriate in professional communications; however, business-related texting is generally limited to the daylight hours. Rwandans also make heavy use of texting, Instagram, and Whatsapp groups to communicate goings-on in the community.

## THE MEDIA
### Press

According to Reporters Without Borders, Rwanda scored 156th place out of 180 countries in its 2018 World Press Freedom Index. The watchdog organization notes that "censorship and self-censorship are ubiquitous in Rwanda," and that "authoritarianism and censorship are likely to continue for the foreseeable future." In his book *Bad News: Last Journalists in a Dictatorship*, Anjan Sundaram offers a scathing indictment of alleged harassment and persecution of journalists within the country who voice criticism of the government.

### "I Heard it on the Grapevine"

Several years ago, I was in Rwanda during Kwibuka—the week of remembrance commemorating the genocide—and I wanted to attend a memorial service to pay my respects, but no one seemed to know when, where, or if such services would occur. In 2017, I was in Rwanda during the presidential election, and I likewise wanted to attend a rally, but no one seemed to know anything in advance. In both instances, however, Rwandans suddenly knew of services and rallies at the eleventh hour—and this thanks to Whatsapp groups, who disseminated the information like wildfire. If you are in Rwanda, therefore, and want to find out about local meetings, ceremonies, or gatherings, ask a Rwandan if they know anything via Whatsapp groups or texting, because they will typically know and share this information long before a Westerner might catch on to it, and much of the information might not be announced until the day before the event.

Whatever the reality, you will find that most media outlets in Rwanda, while they may offer criticism of individual politicians who have somehow fallen into disfavor, will never disseminate a genuine critique of the government or its policies. Much of the news coverage about Rwanda's politics and development will be near obsequious praise.

At the top of the list of Rwandan publications is the *New Times*, available in print and online. Published in English, it mostly offers stories of national interest, as well as op-eds, sports, letters to the editor, and cultural notes. *KT Press* and *News of Rwanda* also offer English-language news, with a similar political slant to the *New Times*. For balanced coverage of national politics you will need to look at those (mostly online) publications created outside Rwanda, such as *Inyenyeri News* and *The Rwandan*. There are a number of Kinyarwanda news publications, including *Umuseke*, *Imvaho Nshya*, and *Muhabura* (also available in English). Newspapers and news magazines are having an ever-growing presence online.

## Television and Radio

Apart from the Internet, the most common medium of communications in Rwanda is undoubtedly radio. As you stroll the streets of Kigali or other cities, you will encounter Rwandans, cell phones held up near their shoulders, listening to streaming radio. Radio is a source of news, talk shows, commentary, and music, with the government-owned Radio Rwanda being the most popular station, followed by a number of other, private stations. Some of the popular radio stations are Kiss FM, Contact FM, Radio 10, and Radio One. The BBC World Service is also accessible at 93.9 FM; V oice of America at 104.3 FM; and Deutsche Welle, at 96 FM.

Purely Rwandan television channels are limited, though the number of television owners is growing. The government-owned RBA (Rwanda Broadcasting Agency, which also owns Radio Rwanda) broadcasts

in Kinyarwanda and English. TV1 touts itself as "the most popular television in Rwanda," while TV10 also offers news and other programs. Beyond Rwandan TV stations, some French channels are often available (France 24, Canal+, and TV5), as is the BBC. To subscribe to a wide range of international channels, Rwandans use DStv, a South African cable company.

### Internet

More than ever, Rwandans are connected online, and often have a social media presence and e-mail. For those who do not have a computer or connection at home, Internet cafés and ICT centers are the most popular means for staying connected. To use one, you pay for an amount of time on a shared computer. ICT centers will often also have printers that you can use for a price per page.

If you visit an ICT center, though, be careful not to leave confidential information on a shared machine. Sometimes customers' sessions are not cleared between users, and downloaded documents can remain on the desktop for others to see. As a precaution, manually clear your session and delete your documents to protect your confidentiality. Never assume that your personal information is safe on a public machine. This is sound advice anywhere.

### Telephones

Land telephone lines are becoming ever rarer in Rwanda as more and more people rely on cell phones for personal and business communications. Many businesses and places of work still use landlines, but it is rare for individuals to have these, especially once you leave the cities. Those who wish to have a fixed-line service must contact the partially government-owned Rwanda Tel, Rwanda's national telecoms agency.

Cell phones are omnipresent in Rwanda and are by far the most common means of communication, using both calls and texting. The largest carrier in Rwanda is MTN, a South African company, whose yellow-and-red parasols dot the roadsides throughout the country. The blue-and-white logoed Tigo is also a large provider, as is Airtel, and RwandaTel.

Cell phone calls are prepaid. After purchasing your device, you must purchase units (*amaunite,* ah-mah-yu-nee-TAY) from one of the many telephone card vendors under the parasols. After agreeing on the number of units you wish to purchase, the vendor will enter a verification code into your phone, which he or she has scratched to reveal from a phone card. You are

then set to call and text
until you have used all of
your units.

The explosion of
cell phone ubiquity has
revolutionized many
aspects of Rwandan
society. On a personal
level, Rwandans use cell
phones not only for voice
calling but for texting,
Internet, radio, and
Mobile Money, which
allows users throughout
Eastern Africa to send

and receive funds wirelessly. For businesspeople,
Mobile Money has eliminated much of the hassle in
doing business. For example, if someone wants to pay
a merchant in Kenya for an import, they no longer
need to go to Western Union or to a bank to wire
funds (which often requires a fee). Now they can
send money directly from person to person.

## MAIL

To send and receive mail, Rwandans must rent a
PO box at a local post office. The Rwandan national
postal service is Iposita, recognizable by its orange,
blue, and white square logo and the yellow façades of
its buildings. Private residences do not have mailing
addresses, though they may have a street address. It

is not uncommon for friends to share a PO box, and businesses are required to have PO boxes. Rwandans may check their mail infrequently, so urgent information should be first communicated via e-mail, phone, or in person. Typically, Rwandans use the post office for mail only.

For mailing packages, DHL and FedEx are reliable carriers in and out of the country. Packages sent from the United States to Rwanda by regular mail do not always arrive, so you should rely on a reputable carrier.

## CONCLUSION

Rwanda was thrust into the world's consciousness in 1994 by a catastrophe of epic proportions: a systematically planned murder of a million men, women, and children. While most of the world turned away, Rwanda became engulfed in hatred, death, and despair for a hundred ill-fated days from April 6 to July 4. As General Roméo Dallaire expressed it in the subtitle of his memoir *Shake Hands With the Devil*, humanity failed Rwanda.

Over the next ten years, Rwanda ebbed and flowed from the world's mind, but slowly, slowly—*buhoro, buhoro*—the Land of a Thousand Hills reemerged in the media. But this time, it was as a country that was not only recovering, but was on the way to becoming a social and economic leader in East Africa, if not the entire continent. The old wounds were many and profound, but Hutu refugees were invited back, a stateless diaspora returned home, and former *génocidaires* reached out to ask forgiveness of those whose lives they had destroyed. A new constitution was drafted, elections were held, and all major economic and social indicators were on the rise. Rwanda had been reborn, and once again tourists and investors arrived, ready to wonder at the majestic beauty of this land and to pour investment dollars into business, ICT, and infrastructure.

Despite the immense suffering and hardship endured by the Rwandan people over much of the last century, Rwandans remain a welcoming and friendly people who are proud of their history, culture, language, and astronomical rebirth after unspeakable horrors. True, there are a number of barriers to your quickly making long-lasting friends in Rwanda: a natural reserve in communication styles and emotions, a challenging language, and Rwandan stereotypes about foreigners who have historically had less-than-altruistic motives in visiting the Land of a Thousand Hills. Building friendships with Rwandans takes time, effort, and trust. It takes a sincere and sustained effort to understand Rwandan culture, to respect it, and to embrace it. Indeed, to truly get to know Rwandans—on their own terms— you must either spend a long time in the country, or return often, making a point of visiting your new acquaintances. Doing so will eventually help these acquaintances to become friends. And once you have made Rwandan friends, you can count on them remaining so for the rest of your life.

# Further Reading

### Nonfiction

Briggs, Philip. *Rwanda, with Eastern Congo (Bradt Travel Guide)*. Bucks: Bradt Travel Guides, 2018.

Carr, Rosamond. *Land of a Thousand Hills: My Life in Rwanda*. New York: Plume, 2000.

Crisafulli, Patricia and Andrea Redmond. *Rwanda, Inc.: How a Devastated Nation Became an Economic Model for the Developing World*. New York: St. Martin's Press, 2012.

Dallaire, Roméo. *Shake Hands with the Devil: The Failure of Humanity in Rwanda*. New York: Carroll and Graf Publishers, 2004.

Hands, Arthur. *A Comprehensive Guide to Kinyarwanda*. Berrien Springs: GEM Resources International, 2013.

Kinzer, Stephen. *A Thousand Hills: Rwanda's Rebirth and the Man Who Dreamed It*. Hoboken: John Wiley & Sons, 2008.

Rusesabagina, Paul. *An Ordinary Man: An Autobiography*. London: Bloomsbury, 2006.

Sebarenzi, Joseph and Laura Mullane. *God Sleeps in Rwanda: A Journey of Transformation*. New York: Atria Books, 2009.

Sommers, Marc. *Stuck: Rwandan Youth and the Struggle for Adulthood*. Athens: The University of Georgia Press, 2012.

Wilkens, Carl. *I'm Not Leaving*. Spokane: World Outside My Shoes, 2011.

### Fiction

Barfuss, Lukas. *One Hundred Days*. London: Granta Books, 2012.

Combres, Elisabeth. *Broken Memory: A Novel of Rwanda*. Toronto: Groundwood Books, 2009.

Crawford, Brian. *The Weaver's Scar: For Our Rwanda*. Unionville: Royal Fireworks Press, 2013.

Mukasonga, Scholastique. *Our Lady of the Nile*. Brooklyn: Archipelago Books, 2014.

Parkin, Gaile. *Baking Cakes in Kigali*. New York: Bantam Books, 2009.

# Sources

In addition to my personal conversations and interviews, the following were important sources for data and facts, especially for the sections on history, traditions, and politics: *L'histoire du Rwanda pré-Nyiginya*, by Bernadin Muzungu (Kigali: Les cahiers Lumière et Société, 2017); *Historical Dictionary of Rwanda, Second Edition*, by Aimable Twagilimana (London: Rowman & Littlefield, 2016); *History and Citizenship for Rwandan Schools, Senior 1*, by Tisaasa Myres, et. al. (Kigali: Longhorn Publishers, Ltd., 2016); *Resilience of a Nation: A History of the Military in Rwanda*, by Frank Rusagara (Kigali: Fountain Publishers, 2009); *Histoire du Rwanda Pré-Colonial*, by Bernardin Muzungu (Paris: L'Harmattan, 2003); The National Ethnographic Musem of Huye (Butare); *Proverbes du Rwanda*, by Pierre Crépeau and Simon Bizimana (Tervuren: Musée Royal de l'Afrique Centrale, 1979; this was my source for the proverb on p. 53; the translation is my own). *Vision 2020* (revised 2012), by The Republic of Rwanda (Kigali, 2012); *2016 Education Statistical Yearbook*, by The Republic of Rwanda Ministry of Education (Kigali, 2016); *The Economic Development and Poverty Reduction Strategy II: 2013-2018*, by The Republic of Rwanda Ministry of Finance and Economic Planning (Kigali, 2013); *The CIA World Factbook* (online).

The Kigali Genocide Memorial museum; as well as the Web sites for the Republic of Rwanda Ministry of Justice, Ministry of Finance and Economic Planning, Ministry of Justice, Ministry of Trade and Industry, Ministry of Education, Ministry of Sports and Culture, and Ministry of Public Service and Labour.

culture smart! rwanda

# Index

# Acknowledgments

As I was researching this book, the following individuals were extremely helpful in sharing their insights about Rwandan culture and etiquette, both in formal interviews and in casual conversations. I would like to thank them immensely for their time and observations on a rich and rewarding culture: Chantal Akayezu; Éric Bizimana; Erin Dees; Clémentine Dusabejambo; Neil Edwards; Claver Hategekimana; Patrick Iradukunda; Paul Karemera; Jacques Kayigema; Cheryl Mutabazi; Steve Mutabazi; Lauren Nkubanda; Lia Preftes; Shelly Rosen; Margo Rukashaza; Matt Stenovec; Sandra Umubyeyi; Jane Usanase; and the many other Rwandans and non-Rwandans who, through informal discussions, explained and commented upon myriad elements of Rwandan culture. Of these, I would particularly like to thank Neil Edwards, Paul Karemera, Shelly Rosen, and Margo Rukashaza, all of whom read my manuscript and provided invaluable suggestions. *Murakoze cyane kumfasha.*